brilliant

how to write a brilliant CV

how to
write a
brilliant
CV

Jim Bright, Joanne Earl
and David Winter

PEARSON

Harlow, England • London • New York • Boston • San Francisco • Toronto • Sydney • Auckland • Singapore • Hong Kong
Tokyo • Seoul • Taipei • New Delhi • Cape Town • São Paulo • Mexico City • Madrid • Amsterdam • Munich • Paris • Milan

PEARSON EDUCATION LIMITED
Edinburgh Gate
Harlow CM20 2JE
United Kingdom
Tel: +44 (0)1279 623623
Web: www.pearson.com/uk

First published in Australia in 2000 by Business + Publishing
First published in Great Britain as *Brilliant CV* in 2001 by Pearson Education
Fifth edition published as *How to Write a Brilliant CV* in 2015 (print and electronic)

© James Bright and Joanne Earl 2000, 2001, 2008, 2011
© James Bright, Joanne Earl and David Winter 2015 (print and electronic)

The rights of James Bright, Joanne Earl and David Winter to be identified as authors of this work
have been asserted by them in accordance with the Copyright, Designs and Patents Act 1988.

Pearson Education is not responsible for the content of third-party internet sites.

ISBN: 978-1-292-01537-8 (print)
      978-1-292-01539-2 (PDF)
      978-1-292-01540-8 (ePub)
      978-1-292-01538-5 (eText)

British Library Cataloguing-in-Publication Data
A catalogue record for the print edition is available from the British Library

Library of Congress Cataloging-in-Publication Data
Bright, Jim.
  [Amazing résumés]
  How to write a brilliant CV / Jim Bright, Joanne Earl and David Winter. -- Fifth edition.
    pages cm
  Earlier editions published as Amazing résumés : what employers want to see--and how to say it.
  Includes bibliographical references and index.
  ISBN 978-1-292-01537-8 (limp : alk. paper)
  1. Résumés (Employment) 2. Job hunting. I. Title.
  HF5383.B69 2015
  650.14'2--dc23

Series cover design: David Carroll & Co.

Print edition typeset in 10.5pt Plantin Std by 30
Print edition printed by Ashford Colour Press Ltd, Gosport

NOTE THAT ANY PAGE CROSS REFERENCES REFER TO THE PRINT EDITION

For Beryl Bright, her sister Sylvia Cox and their mother Violet Parsons –
three very special women

and for David and Brenda Earl

and for David's brilliant wife Susanna.

Contents

About the authors

Jim Bright (BA, PhD, FAPS, FCDAA, MNCDA, FNICEC Reg. Psychologist) was born in Royal Leamington Spa. He has a degree and PhD in Psychology from the University of Nottingham. Jim has lived and worked in Australia since 1995. He is the owner of a career management firm, Bright and Associates (**www.brightandassociates.com.au**) where he provides coaching, career and medico-legal assessment and training to individuals, companies and fellow professionals. His clients include many national and international companies and he works around the world. Jim is the author of many other career books including *The Chaos Theory of Careers*.

Jim holds the positions of Professor of Career Education and Development at the Australian Catholic University and Visiting Professor in Career Development at the University of Derby, UK. He has published many peer-reviewed journal articles on careers in leading scientific journals. In addition, each year he presents at leading national and international scientific conferences in the area of careers and management. He is a regular guest on radio and television and is frequently quoted in international media. Jim also writes a weekly column on careers in the *Sydney Morning Herald*, as well as hosting a careers blog called *The Factory* at **www.brightandassociates.com.au/wordpress** and tweets as @DrJimBright.

In his spare time, Jim enjoys jazz music and cricket. He can be contacted at **www.brightandassociates.com.au**.

Joanne Earl (BEd, BA, MPsychol [Applied], PhD, MAPS) is a registered psychologist and a member of the Australian Psychological Society (APS), the APS College of Organisational Psychologists and the Australian Association of Career Counsellors. She has more than 20 years' experience working in various human resources, training and psychological consulting roles. She is now a Senior Lecturer in Psychology in the School of Psychology, University of New South Wales. Her research interests focus on organisational psychology and include career planning across the life cycle, accuracy of self-rated abilities and whether being decided about a career really matters to important work outcomes.

David Winter has been a careers consultant at the University of London for nearly 20 years and has lost count of the number of CVs he has looked at in that time. He has worked with undergraduates, postgraduates and graduates of all ages from a wide range of disciplines. He also provides career and leadership coaching and training to mid-career professionals. In addition, on behalf of The Careers Group, University of London, he has provided consultancy and training to a variety of employers on effective recruitment and selection of graduates.

Acknowledgements

There have been many organisational psychologists, human resource managers and recruitment consultants who have provided us with great assistance in writing this book. We would like to thank Fiona Davies, Prue Laurence, Sonia Hutton (now Manser), Dimitra Papadolias, Sharon Wilkenfeld, Emma Lee, Lynne Clune and Erin Stephenson, whose Masters and Honours research on CVs has provided us with invaluable help. Robert Bright was the human resources expert who started this all off – characteristically over a curry – with the simple question: 'What do we really know for sure about CVs?'

Jenny Reddin and KODAK Pty Ltd supported our early work. Our research was helped tremendously by Dr Rob Anderson, Rachel Kenny and Jennifer Blake. Special thanks to Ms Doreen Cheong, who has guided our thinking on electronic CVs and co-presented seminars on this topic with us. Kevin Chandler ex Chandler and Macleod Pty Ltd assisted us with their search on photographs and web-based recruitment. Many human resource professionals in Sydney and Melbourne aided us by participating in our studies and reading through all the different CVs. Thanks to all our colleagues who have encouraged us in this project by reviewing our journal articles and even awarding us prizes!

The School of Psychology at the University of New South Wales (UNSW) has supported these studies and many of the staff there have provided useful feedback to us on the processes. Thanks to our collaborator Dr Austin Adams for his generous help. More recently the School of Education at the Australian Catholic University has supported Jim's work.

Thanks to Audrey Chung for her contributions to earlier versions and to Tim Edwards who developed the original project. Thanks to Allen and Unwin for their support for many years.

Finally, thanks to the publishing team at Pearson Education including Eloise Cook and Steve Temblett.

Introduction

Remember your first date, or the first time you went out with your partner? Did you make sure your clothes were right, your hair was perfect, you were wearing the right perfume or aftershave? Well, at least that much effort should go into getting your CV right! CVs are 'first dates' in the selection process that could land you on a new career path. Like the first date, they are the first time an employer gets to form an opinion about you – and first impressions can make all the difference. Employers routinely receive thousands of CVs from candidates seeking the same job. That can mean odds of 1,000 to 1 or even worse. A bad CV can reduce those chances from a long-shot of 1,000 to 1 to 0. A well thought-out CV can boost the same candidate's chance of being interviewed to 1 in 3. Think about it: just by changing your CV, you can go from a situation where no-one would interview you to being interviewed on every third occasion. In some cases we are able to boost a CV so that the candidate is always interviewed.

In our experience with career transition clients, they tend to focus their nervous energy on the interview. Perhaps because the interview is closer to the final decision point, people think it is more important. However, it turns out that the interview is no more important in predicting the final decision. We compared the importance of the CV with the interview in determining overall candidate suitability. The CV provides most data on competencies and achievements (or should if properly written), whereas the interview provides more data on interpersonal skills and rapport. CVs count! You must put as much effort into your CV as you do into your interview.

Getting a job today can involve several steps, starting with a CV, followed by psychological tests and interviews. The CV is the only step where you have control over the information that you present. In every other step, the employer decides what questions to ask, what information to collect. The CV is your vital opportunity to present yourself at your best. CVs are important.

There are many different books on the market providing advice on CV preparation. This is the first book that gives clear, down-to-earth advice that has been shown to work scientifically. This book is the culmination of years of scientific research into what makes a winning (and losing) CV. We have interviewed hundreds of recruiters across a wide spectrum of industries and asked them to judge real CVs. The advice we now pass on to you is based on sound principles that have emerged from this work and from the peer-reviewed research work of others around the world, and not on gossip, hearsay or anecdotes.

The aim of this guide is to provide you with no-nonsense advice about how to get the most out of your CV. It will increase your chances of being shortlisted for that all-important job.

We show you how to put together a persuasive CV. We give examples of CVs that work and those that don't and we explain to you why one works and another doesn't. We introduce you to some key job-seeking skills that will improve the quality of your CV. Every person has different strengths and weaknesses. The authors of *How to Write a Brilliant CV* are organisational psychologists and careers experts who understand these differences. Using simple exercises, we will show you how to tailor a CV to your strengths.

In the following chapters, we provide advice on the layout, content and construction of your CV and its covering letter. We also address some of the tricky questions:

- Do I explain gaps in my career history?
- Do I need different CVs for different jobs?
- Should I describe all my duties at work?
- Can I email my CV?
- Can I get any clues from the job advertisement that will improve my CV?

- Do I include a photograph?
- Can I leave stuff out of my CV and, if so, what stuff?

We are confident that this guide will assist you in producing the best possible CV. The recruitment industry has assisted us in all of our work, and the advice we pass on here is a reflection of our close relationship with the people who are making decisions about CVs every day. The results of our work have been published in several industry and international scientific journals, and have been presented at international conferences in Australia and the USA. Training courses based on our work have been conducted in blue-chip companies.

How to use this book

How to Write a Brilliant CV is divided into four parts. Part 1 introduces the concept of a CV as a marketing document, and leads the reader through a series of exercises to help them put together a thorough CV. Part 2 builds on this by showing how they can enhance their CV to make it even stronger. Part 3 provides answers to some of those tricky questions regarding what to include and what to leave out, as well as issues such as referees, dealing with prejudice, the recruiter's thought processes during selection and using the internet. Finally, Part 4 provides a series of valuable resources to assist you in the preparation of your CVs and some useful sources for getting more information on jobs and CVs.

Throughout this book you will see 'Brilliant tips' in boxes. All of these tips come straight from the human resource experts we interviewed and surveyed in our research programme, so you know exactly what the experts want to see! Throughout, and in the last section especially, you will see graphs, figures and tables that report data that have come straight from our studies, so at all times you are getting facts to back up the advice given.

Notes on the latest edition

We are delighted with the continuing success of this book, which continues to be a best-selling CV guide in the UK. It also has proved popular in the

USA, Australia, China and Vietnam, to name a few countries, and we continually receive emails from readers from right around the globe. We are convinced the success of this book is based upon the sound scientific evidence that we have collected and continue to collect, which informs all of the advice given. It is what sets this book apart from all of the others and, judging by the outstanding success stories we hear from our readers who have followed our model, we are doing something right.

The internet is a great source of information about job vacancies, but it has a long way to go to supersede the convenience of the humble CV. Furthermore, the internet has spawned a lot of total rubbish masquerading as advice to job hunters. If you followed some of this advice (and some of it appears on leading job websites) you could irreparably harm your job prospects. It is worth reflecting that free advice often has the same value – i.e. it is worthless!

Imitation is the sincerest form of flattery, and thus we are most flattered that there now exist publications that have 'incorporated' much of the advice and ideas that we have been presenting for the last decade. Ultimately what matters is that you, the job hunter, are given information that has been demonstrated to be effective, and so it is heartening that others see the value in our work and see fit to incorporate it in their own. Issues relating to layout, the analysis of job advertisements in a systematic manner, the use of competency statements, the inclusion of narrative and the metaphor of dating as a model of job hunting have all found their way into the advice now routinely provided to job hunters.

A word about evidence-based and experience-based approaches to job hunting: when we wrote the first edition of *Brilliant CV* we were unaware of any guides that were based upon proper behavioural studies of résumé short-listing. Most books at the time (and still to this day) are simply the opinions of people who claim experience in the field. While experience is useful, it is necessarily narrow and somewhat arbitrary. More recently some imitators have taken to doing surveys asking recruiters what they like to see in a résumé. The trouble with this method is, that what people tell you they will do and what they actually do, can be two very different things. For this reason we went to much greater trouble to set up experiments where recruiters undertook short-listing exercises unaware that we had carefully manipulated and controlled the résumés they read. By doing this we could see which résumés containing which features were actually short-listed. We also gained access to thousands of real résumés linked to real employment outcomes and carefully analysed the differences between the short-listed ones and the rejected ones. The advice in this book goes way beyond surveys and informal chats with recruiters – and it is far more rigorous and reliable as a result. We wish that more research was done to help job hunters and that more CV guides were truly evidence-based.

Of course we must declare a bias, and say that we think getting information from our particular horse's mouth is still your best bet! We continue to be actively interested in what best helps the job hunter and to that end we have added yet more material to assist you in navigating an increasingly complex, turbulent and unpredictable labour market.

We are thrilled that David has joined the team. David is Head of Corporate Consultancy at The Careers Group, University of London. David has an enviable reputation in the career development world and has led the development of the first careers and employability massive open online course (MOOC) for the University of London, helping over 70,000 people from around the world to take more control of their career development.

We have adapted and rewritten most of the book. Some of the highlights in this edition include:

- specific CV examples
- updated CV research and advice based on the best available peer-reviewed research
- alternative makeover CVs to allow you to choose between different styles reflecting different CV-writing techniques
- updated and online resources
- a brand new approach to writing narratives on your CV – a clever technique that serves as a script for your interview.

In fact there are far too many changes to list here, so the best thing to do is to dive in and start improving your CV right now!

PART 1

Writing a CV from scratch

The first part of the book is designed to take you through some of the fundamental stages in putting together your CV. It will be particularly useful for readers who have never attempted to construct a CV before, or for those who have not done so recently. Of course, even if you have a basic CV, it never hurts to revisit first principles to ensure you are building from a strong foundation.

CHAPTER 1

How to sell yourself

ndy Warhol said everybody gets their 15 minutes of fame. The CV is your opportunity to be in the spotlight, but unfortunately most candidates are lucky to get five minutes. It depends on the job and the number of applicants, but recruiters will, on average, spend less than two minutes reading a CV. They'll never admit it publicly, but it is not unheard of for a recruiter to send a CV straight to the waste-paper basket with nothing more than a quick glance.

Your job is to make the most of that tiny window of opportunity to sell yourself to the recruiter. Your CV must sell, sell, sell! It must sell you.

brilliant tip

Remember that you are marketing yourself so, while the integrity of the document is a must, the CV must present your best experience and detail your relevant skills and competencies.

Standing tall

Some people come over all shy and retiring when we tell them to present themselves at their best. For many people, it is not natural to be forth-coming and assertive. Our language is stacked with words and phrases that reflect this concern – 'blowing your own trumpet', 'bighead', 'up yourself'!

The fact of the matter is, you have to sell yourself. Do not think that employers will run to your door, overcome and enchanted by your modesty and understatement.

Still not convinced? Just consider all the other applicants. Will they be equally timid? You have to make your CV better than theirs. You have to make yourself better than them.

Hands up how many of you are thinking: 'Oh no, I'm being asked to go way over the top, and that's not me!'

Remember, there are even more ways of selling things than there are ways of skinning cats (and most of them are a lot less noisy).

> ## brilliant tip
>
> Don't lay out your life, warts and all, and expect a recruiter to be able to pick through your story, see your inherent skills and marvel at your honesty.

Consider the following three approaches to your CV.

Not selling yourself – too negative

'I did not enjoy college so I deferred and travelled around for a couple of years. I got to see a lot of different countries but eventually returned home, and I am now seeking a job …'

Good selling – turning negatives into believable positives

'After enrolling at college I was provided with an opportunity to join a crew sailing around the world. I accepted this once-in-a-lifetime challenge, which offered me invaluable lessons in the importance of teamwork, shared responsibility and leadership. I am now seeking to apply these skills …'

Bad selling – way over the top, unbelievable and undesirable

'I found I was not sufficiently challenged by the intellectual rigour of college life and left to pursue more appropriate ventures. I masterminded a round-the-world

yacht race and, although there were other crew on board, most would probably agree I was the leader. I can now do wonders for you ...'

The purpose of checking these three approaches against your CV is to make the point that you should not confuse selling yourself with telling lies, wild exaggeration or deliberately misleading someone.

Selling yourself is about being positive and persuading others to share this view of you.

Suppose you are driving with a friend as a passenger who is getting impatient and wants to know when you'll arrive at your destination. You are halfway there. What do you say to soothe them? If the journey were two miles, then saying, 'Only another one mile to go' would sound better than, 'We're only halfway there'. If the journey were 2,000 miles in total, which would sound better: 'Only another 1,000 miles to go', or 'We're halfway there already'?

Neither statement is untrue, nor misleading, but one serves your purpose well and the other does not. It is the same with CV writing.

brilliant tip

If you cannot say something in a positive way, consider not saying it at all.

But how positive?

So, selling is important. That said, remember that selling is like perfume – a little used judiciously is attractive and enhances the person, but drown yourself in perfume and it is a big turn-off! The same goes for selling yourself: you need to know when to stop.

The following chapters will go into detail about how best to sell yourself but, before we move on, test yourself on our Over-the-top quiz.

Over-the-top quiz

Rate each of the ideas using the scale below:

1 The work of a sad and deranged mind.

2 Not me, but I know someone who would.

3 Hmm, sounds interesting, tell me more.

4 Who gave you a copy of my CV?

Make your CV stand out by using brightly coloured paper and a really *wacky font*	1	2	3	4
Get your CV delivered by a bikini-clad woman	1	2	3	4
If you are a bank manager, set out your CV like a cheque-book	1	2	3	4
If you are an architect, design your CV in 3-D, in the form of a house	1	2	3	4
If going for a job in advertising, attach a condom to your CV ('I'm a SAFE bet …')	1	2	3	4

Now add your points and check your score. How did you do?

4–5 points You will lead a long, happy and successful life. You were not tempted by these way over-the-top ways of getting a recruiter's attention. These approaches nearly always fail, despite any rumours you may have heard.

6–10 points You are not a bad person, but you have some strange friends or are easily led. Good to see you would not use these methods, but you could offer to rewrite the CVs of those who might be tempted.

11–15 points Get help urgently! The help you need can be found below in the section on wacky CVs. Read it carefully and follow the advice.

16–20 points To quote from *The Life of Brian*: 'It is people like you wot cause unrest.' Read the following section carefully and, for the sake of your job application, trust us, the wacky way is not the successful way.

The wacky CV

We have seen and heard of plenty of different 'way-out' CVs and, without exception, we would never recommend them. Don't be tempted, not even for a minute. Some of you might be saying, 'Well, what's wrong with that idea?', or possibly, 'But you haven't read my CV!' Let's look at each in turn.

A CV delivered by a bikini-clad woman

If you were going for a job as doorman in the Playboy Club circa 1975, this might just be a good move. Come on!

Anyone using a semi-clad woman to advance their application probably will be written off as insensitive and coarse at best, and a misogynist and chauvinist at worst. Questions of appropriateness and targeting the particular requirements of the position are discussed later.

Bank manager's CV set out like a cheque-book

When has being a raging individualist been a prerequisite for working in a bank? A recruiter might ask themselves why a bank manager needed to use gimmicks: what are they hiding? (And how would I get it in the photocopier?)

Architect's 3-D CV in the form of a house

This is a bit more understandable but, again, the candidate is risking appearing a bit twee or lightweight. And, of course, there are practical problems for recruiters receiving these sorts of CVs. How do they file or copy them easily?

Advertising candidate CV with condom attached

Please!

Using coloured paper or unusual fonts

In a study we conducted with recruiters, all of them hated the unusual CV we showed them – it was on coloured paper and printed with a strange font. When we presented the same CV on white paper in a standard font, all the recruiters were impressed (see Figure 1.1). What is more, they said the unusual CV contained less information, even though the content was the same as the more conventional CV. Recruiters may not even read your pimped up CV!

Findings from other recent independent studies support our results. A recent European study[1] suggests that using a formal versus a creative CV layout almost doubles the applicant's chance of being shortlisted. The advice is clear – use elaborate fonts and be creative with layout at your peril.

You will hear stories of people getting interviews and jobs that they think they got by using gimmicky CVs. These are exceptional cases – do not be tempted.

Taste test

So, why do recruiters dislike 'wacky' CVs? The answers could fill another book, but there are some examples in life that reinforce this view. First, there is good old taste. A painting by Picasso may be a great work of art to one person, and worse than a child's scribble to another. People's tastes differ. Many people tend to like things that are familiar.

Secondly, people's opinions differ. Just think about politics and sport. In most countries there are two or three political parties that have widespread support and then lots of 'minority interest' parties. Think about the arguments that rage about the selection of sportsmen and women to national teams. How does all this relate to CVs? All we are saying here is that things that are unusual will attract attention – like a Picasso painting or an unusual decision by a selector – and in return will elicit a reaction, positive or negative. If you don't know how the reader will react, why run the risk of rejection unnecessarily?

---

[1] Arnulf, J.K., Tegner, L. Larssen, Ø., 'Impression making by résumé layout: Its impact on the probability of being shortlisted', *European Journal of Work and Organizational Psychology*, 2010, 19 (2), 221–230.

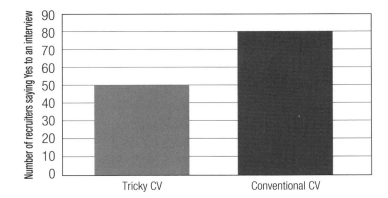

Figure 1.1 Recruiters' responses to unusual CVs

brilliant tip

Never be tempted to use an unusual layout, no matter what stories of success you hear.

CHAPTER 2

The applicant—
employer fit

What is fit?

If you hang around with recruitment consultants for long enough (about two minutes is usually adequate) you will hear them talking about 'fit'. The way that they see recruitment and the way many firms think about it is in terms of getting a good 'fit' between the employer and the employee. Figure 2.1 illustrates this concept of fit.

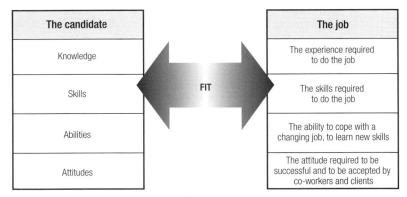

Figure 2.1 Factors in finding the right fit

As you can see from the diagram, fit is all about matching a candidate to a particular job. The best candidate for the job will be the one who matches all the requirements of the position.

You can also see from Figure 2.1 that employers tend to think about 'fit' in terms of four different qualities:

1   *Knowledge* which refers to the experience and qualifications that you possess.

2   *Skills* which refers to the demonstrated skills you have (perhaps evidenced by your qualifications).

3   *Abilities* which show your potential to carry out a range of different tasks beyond your immediate skills or knowledge, and the degree to which you can take on new tasks successfully or be trained in new methods or equipment.

4   *Attitudes* which indicate your personality, and the degree to which you are enthusiastic, flexible and positive in approach.

It is clear when you look at Figure 2.1 that merely setting out your life history on a CV is highly unlikely to offer the best fit. This is why it is so important to tailor your CV to the particular position – to increase the fit between you and the job.

The following example illustrates this point.

Applicants for a sales assistant job in a chemist

	Job requirements	Tim	Liz	Jane
Knowledge	Knows how a cash register works. Knows procedures for dealing with customers	*Degree in English, worked part-time in a burger bar for 18 months*	*Worked in father's hardware store for 6 years*	*Worked in a shoe shop for 3 years*
Skills	Numeracy. Good communication skills	*Easily able to handle cash and card transactions*	*Easily able to handle cash and card transactions*	*Easily able to handle cash and card transactions*
Abilities	To learn to process charge cards, electronic transactions	*No difficulties learning new skills*	*No evidence of learning new skills*	*Probably able to deal with new payment methods with some training*
Attitudes	Polite, punctual, trustworthy, calm	*Strong-minded, self-confident, assertive*	*Honest, a bit aloof at times*	*Calm, honest, level-headed*
Degree of fit		POOR	AVERAGE	GOOD

▶ brilliant example

Three candidates have applied for a sales job. From reading their CVs, the employer has listed each candidate's knowledge, skills and abilities on a grid, next to the job requirements. Which candidate fits the job best?

We think that Tim is the weakest candidate. He has the best academic qualifications, but these are unnecessary for the position offered. Although Tim could easily learn new skills and accommodate changing demands in the job, the comment in Tim's CV, 'I am a strong-minded person who is not afraid to stand my ground in disputes', gave an unfortunate impression of someone who might be argumentative with the public.

Liz clearly has a lot of experience in retail, but in a very different area. There could be some concerns about her ability to deal with customers sensitively. There did not appear to be much development of new skills over the six years, and little evidence that she would adapt to new payment processes easily.

Jane looks the strongest candidate to us. She has the necessary experience, and should be able to adapt to most new processes with training. She is not over- or under-qualified for the job and seems the best prospect.

In this analysis you might think we have been terribly unfair to one or other of the candidates. Perhaps we have, but the point of this example is to illustrate the sorts of processes that recruiters go through in making decisions to short-list applicants.

✦ brilliant tip

Make sure your CV addresses the advertised position.

Improving the fit

When you set out job requirements as clearly as this, it is easy to see how you can start to mould your CV to match the job. Each of the candidates above probably could make themselves look the best candidate by altering their CVs. Below we offer some advice and we describe these changes in more detail in the following chapters.

Tim could turn that negative remark about standing his ground into a positive, by rephrasing it: 'I have received feedback from previous managers about my confidence in dealing with a wide range of customers and my ability to help them make the right decision.' Tim could also put more emphasis on his retail experience and less on his education. Perhaps a 'career objective' statement outlining what Tim hopes to achieve would help persuade the recruiter that this would be a serious career move for him.

Liz needs to make far more of her six years of experience. There must be many achievements and new skills that she has learned. These need to be emphasised on the CV. Jane looks pretty good already, but perhaps she could try to emphasise her abilities, or her potential to learn more, by providing examples of new skills she has learned over the past three years.

So now you've seen that CVs need to sell, and you know how recruiters use the best 'fit' as a guide to the best candidate. The next chapter shows you how to work out what recruiters are looking for – how to determine the job's requirements.

brilliant tips

1   If it increases the fit between you and the job, put it in the CV and say it in the interview.

2   If it decreases the fit between you and the job, omit it from the CV and don't say it in the interview.

3   If it is neutral or you are not sure of the fit, only include it if there is room and only say it if there is time.

CHAPTER 3

Where is the
prime suspect?

Becoming a job detective

Imagine the scene: an office in the City, but there is someone missing from one desk. Witnesses say the missing person is motivated, well qualified and pays exceptional attention to detail ...

Every employer has a 'prime suspect' in mind when they advertise a position, and they tend to leave clues to that person's identity in their job descriptions. In this chapter we teach you to become a job detective, so that you can pick up all the clues and solve the mystery – what would the ideal candidate for this job look like?

To produce the best 'fitting' CV you need to know about yourself and you need to know about the job you are applying for. This chapter shows you how to work out exactly what the job is all about, and the following chapters then show you how best to mould your CV to the job to produce the best fit.

brilliant tip

CVs should always be written with the job in mind.

Job detectives question themselves

Before you do anything else, ask yourself why you are preparing a CV. The answer to this question is going to vary from one person to the next, but here are our top 10 reasons for writing a CV.

Top 10 reasons for writing a CV

1 You have seen a job advertised that appeals to you.

2 You want to market yourself to win a tender or a proposal, or be elected to a committee or organisation.

3 You are thinking about moving on from your current job and this helps you to summarise where you are at now.

4 Your friends/family told you of a job going at East West Ltd.

5 You want to work for East West Ltd and thought that sending a CV to them might get their attention.

6 You have seen a job advertised internally at work.

7 You are going for promotion.

8 You are about to be made redundant and want to update your CV to be ready for any good opportunities.

9 You are feeling fed up and writing down all your achievements will cheer you up and might motivate you to look for a better job.

10 Oh, so that's a CV! I've never done one. I suppose I ought to try to remember what I've been doing with my life!

All of these certainly are good reasons to write a CV, but the CV serves many different purposes. One way of seeing the differences is to ask yourself, who is going to read the CV in each case?

- CVs 1 to 5 are going to be read by potential employers who probably do not know you.

- A CV for 6 or 7 is likely to be read by your boss or other people who know you.

- CVs 8 to 10 are really for your own benefit and should not be considered as suitable for sending out to employers.

The right mix

Have a think about the list of reasons again. How else can you divide up these reasons? A most important difference is that, in some cases, you will have a good idea of what the employer is looking for because you have a job advertisement in front of you and can tailor your CV accordingly. For others, you have no idea what the reader might want to see.

It is always worth updating your CV from time to time so you do not forget important details but, remember, the result of that process will not be a winning CV. It will be a useful list of tasks and achievements.

Writing CVs is like baking cakes. You need all the right ingredients: flour, butter, eggs and so on. It is what you do with the ingredients that makes the difference between a great CV (or cake) and failure. Keeping your CV up to date is like keeping a stock of ingredients in the pantry – potentially very useful, but do not imagine that is the end of it.

If there is a most important piece of advice to give you, it is that you must think about what the employer is looking for and then reflect that in your CV. This advice was the most common tip from a large sample of recruitment managers.

brilliant tip

Think about what the employer is looking for and then reflect that in your CV.

CV writing

You should tailor the information in your CV to the main points in the job advertisement. Okay, that sounds fine, but how do I do it?

Get as much information about the job and the company as you can. When you've got that, go and get some more! The main source of information about a job is normally from:

- a job advertisement
- a job description
- a friend in the company
- the media, e.g. Facebook, LinkedIn
- gossip and rumour
- someone already doing the job or something similar.

There is no substitute for experience. Talking to someone who does a job similar to the one you wish to apply for in the same company may well provide you with a good picture of what the job is really like. Bear in mind, of course, that this source of information is not always reliable. You may react differently to your friend, and therefore their experience of a company may be very different from yours.

However, a friend with reliable knowledge can be a golden opportunity. Make sure you do not waste the chance to get some information. One way of ensuring that the information you get is useful is to use our job advertisement interrogation questions on page 30.

brilliant tip

If you have friends who can provide valuable information – use them!

The main source of information about an employer's company is normally from:

- the media
- annual reports/company brochures
- industry/trade magazines or journals
- the internet
- industry directories
- gossip and rumour.

There are many other sources of information about companies and if you're serious about knowing more about a potential employer (and you should be) it's worth a visit to your local library. Ask a reference librarian to help you with your search. It will help if you outline to the librarian that you are looking for information on a specific company to help with your job search.

Understanding an employer's WIIFT

When thinking about any employer, you should always be thinking about how they will see you and what benefits they may see in hiring you. This is known in the trade as the WIIFT, or What's In It For Them.

Understanding the company helps you to better understand the WIIFT, that is, the benefits of having you as an employee.

brilliant tip

Do your homework prior to applying. Find out about the company, obtain an annual report if available, find out what future projects the company might be involved with, who its clients are and who its competitors are.

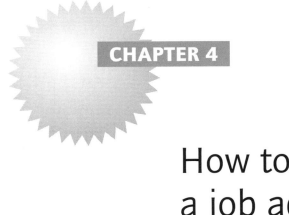

CHAPTER 4

How to read a job ad

The job detective examines the job advert

Job advertisements and descriptions should be treated as clues. Job advertisements are usually reliable sources of information and should be taken seriously. Employers can be found to have broken the law if they put misleading or incorrect information in advertisements.

Information from other sources can sometimes be invaluable, sometimes grossly inaccurate. The same principles apply whatever the source of the information.

Here is a typical job ad. Below it are our tips for reading the ad.

After reading the job advertisement, the following seven questions will assist in breaking down the job ad successfully. Remember, reading an ad properly is the crucial first step to preparing a successful CV.

Training Manager
Handle Sisters Pharmaceuticals

Would you like to join the world's third biggest pharmaceutical company, currently expanding rapidly in the European market? We require a manager to join our training division, where you would be responsible for the delivery of training programmes to our sales staff.

A motivated, results-focused team player, you will have excellent communication skills, and will be able to handle pressure and work to deadlines. With several years of solid experience in a multinational, you will be accredited in NLP and will have a basic understanding of training evaluation techniques. Reporting to our Regional Manager, you will be required to provide input into the marketing strategies for the European region by training our sales staff to improve market share.

Handle Sisters are Equal Opportunity employers.

Please forward your CV to: Linda Spark, Personnel Dept, Handle Sisters Pharmaceuticals, 58 Boundary Street, London EC1 2LP.

The seven job advertisement interrogation questions

1   What don't you understand about the job ad?

2   What type of industry/company is it? What's happening in the company or industry? Is it restructuring or expanding? Does it operate with low overheads and high profit margins?

3   What is the main purpose of the role being offered?

4   Why is this role important to the company? How will this role affect the company's bottom line?

5   What types of skills do they want? What other skills might be needed, given the job's purpose?

6   What types of personal qualities do they want? What other personal qualities might be needed, given the job's purpose?

7   What types of knowledge/training do they want? What other knowledge or training might be needed, given the job's purpose?

Now that you have read the questions, we will take you through them one at a time.

1   What don't you understand about the job ad?

Obviously, you have to make sure that you understand any of the specific technical words or jargon in the job advert, such as 'equal opportunities employer' and 'NLP'. If you are applying for a role in your current field, then this shouldn't be too much of a problem. Although, unfamiliar jargon may indicate that, even if the job title is familiar, perhaps it is being used by this employer to describe a very different role. If you are attempting to change careers, unfamiliar jargon may be a sign that you haven't done enough research yet.

You could search the internet for definitions but you may find it more useful to talk to people already in the industry so that they can explain what it means in practice.

The main thing is to make sure you have understood the role. For example, this advert says you will be 'responsible for the delivery of training programmes'. Does that mean you will deliver the training yourself or that you will have to make sure the training is delivered by coordinating other people, or a bit of both? Will you just be organising the delivery of an existing programme or will you be involved in deciding what the programme should include?

The advert also says 'you will be required to provide input into the marketing strategies for the European region by training our sales staff to increase market share'. Will you be expected to implement a strategy that has already been decided or will you have some input into that strategy? How much will you be held accountable for the increase in market share?

Some of these questions may be answered if the recruiter provides more information in the form of a more detailed job description and person specification. If not, you may need to try to clarify these questions with the employer before you submit an application.

2 What type of industry or company is it and what's happening currently?

Some of this information can be gleaned from the job ad. In our example, the company seems to operate on a global scale as it refers to the 'European division' and asks for experience in multinationals. Secondly, it gives the impression it is expanding in that part of the world. However, this doesn't mean that it is expanding everywhere, and it doesn't say whether Europe includes the UK, where the correspondence address is. The job may involve overseas travel, or be based overseas. It is not possible to tell whether the company is restructuring or what its profitability is.

Information about companies can be gleaned from many different sources. Remember our earlier tip to visit your local library to review any existing information in such publications as *Financial Times Top 500 Companies*. Ask a librarian how best to conduct your search. It is easy to miss huge chunks of information.

Do you know anyone who works for the company? If so, talk to them. Could they get hold of any company brochures, newsletters or advertising material for you? In our example, you might ask whether there is anything in the latest pharmaceutical trade journals.

If you are keen to work for a large company, start reading the business pages of the newspaper to see whether there are any stories about the company. If it is a public company, you could always ask for a copy of the annual report. This may tell you whether the company is growing or not, how profitable it is, and whether any redundancies are planned.

Because this company sells pharmaceuticals, it might be worth going to a pharmacy to ask about the company, or asking a doctor. Then you might be able to find out whether this company sells medicinal products. Also check out the supermarkets to see whether this company sells domestic products such as soap powder. Take the job ad with you, so you can match the logo and address with the products on the shelf.

3   What is the main purpose of the role?

In this case, it is fairly clear that the main duty will be to conduct training of sales staff. Duties are likely to be fairly well known by job applicants, as the role needs somebody with experience and qualifications. However, training itself is a broad role that may involve many responsibilities. It may be that the company specialises in an industry that has very specific training needs. For example, a petroleum company may have to adhere to occupational health and safety (OHS) requirements for using chemicals. Alternatively, training may involve stress management techniques in a high-pressure work environment. It is well worth finding out what particular needs a company may have over and above those in the job advertisement.

4   Why is this role important to the company?

The role is important because the company wants to increase sales of its products. To do so, it thinks it needs better trained sales staff. The company will be looking for someone who can demonstrate an impact on sales through improved training. One way of thinking about this is to ask what problems would result if no one did the job or if they did it badly.

5   What types of skills do they want and what other skills might be needed?

The company wants someone who can teach NLP. Other than that, you will need to be able to gauge whether the company's training programme is successful or not (evaluation). Other skills required are good communication skills. In this job, this involves being able to talk to groups of trainees, produce clear training materials and write reports and present them to management. Because the company is linking the job to strategic planning, it will be important that you are able to demonstrate general business and commercial awareness. Be sure you can find your way around a balance sheet.

6   What personal qualities do they want and what other qualities might be needed?

They want someone who is 'motivated' – meaning somebody who can motivate the sales staff and conduct interesting training courses, and generally make an enthusiastic addition. Communication and team player skills mean you need to get on well with others, speak (in public) well and write well.

7   What knowledge and training do they want and what other knowledge/training might be needed?

A degree in psychology, business or commerce may be useful. Any evidence of business-related experience is probably very useful. Experience in a similar job would be good. The ability to speak a relevant language, such as French, German or Spanish, or experience working in European cultures should improve your chances.

You can see already how, in answering these questions, we are building up a picture of the type of job on offer, and the sort of qualities the candidate should possess. Therefore, we are increasing the chances of a good fit.

You become the job detective

Below is a series of job advertisements. Have a read through each advertisement and make your own list of answers to the job interrogation questions, building your own picture of what the employer wants to see in a candidate. We have completed the first exercise for you.

exercise 1   A worked example

Admin assistant

Due to expansion, an exciting opportunity exists for a person to assist the Administration Manager in a wide variety of work such as marketing mail-outs, customer relations and all other aspects of administration. Applicants must possess good communication skills with the ability to work under pressure during peak workload times. Knowledge of Word and Excel essential. Package negotiable.

Send CV to:

Human Resources Director
Britannia Insurance
PO Box 32
London
NW1 3UL

Let's take a look at the job and examine it together.
We'll start with:

1   **What don't you understand about the job ad?**

So why is this an 'exciting opportunity'?

Did the previous post-holder quickly move on to bigger and better things in this organisation? Perhaps this organisation recruits people for low-level jobs and then tries to develop their potential.

In this case they will be looking not just for your ability to do the job but also for your potential beyond the job.

Perhaps, instead, 'exciting' just means it is a really busy job where you are constantly running from one task to the next. In this case they will be looking for someone tireless and energetic.

2   **What type of industry or company is it?**

These insurance brokers are expanding, but it is not clear whether just the one department is expanding or the whole company is expanding. A search at www.euromoney.com will help you to work out what's happening with the company.

3   **What is the main purpose of the role?**

The main purpose of the job is administration – mail, maybe drafting correspondence, typing (using Word), filing, perhaps keeping diaries for managers, co-ordinating meetings, travel and maybe working with spreadsheets (in Excel), marketing mail-outs and dealing with customers.

4   **Why is this role important to the company?**

The role is to assist the Administration Manager to process administration efficiently and effectively. Any company lives and dies on its efficiency and without an effective administration system professionally run by competent staff, profits will be seriously affected. Your role is to help the Administration Manager make this run smoothly.

5   **What types of skills do they want?**

Communication skills: you are likely to draft correspondence and will need to have good verbal communications to follow instructions. Time management skills: companies tend to run under time constraints, so time management skills will help you be effective in your role. Organisational skills: to help organise the company's administration you will need to be organised yourself! Customer relations: in this role you will be dealing with queries, coping with complaints and managing problems the Administration Manager cannot deal with. You will need to be understanding, patient and diplomatic.

6   **What types of personal qualities do they want?**

This role is clearly a support role, so reliability, punctuality, good organisational skills and attention to detail will all be highly regarded. Given that you are dealing with the public and have to work under pressure, somebody who is polite and not too hot-headed would probably be well regarded.

7   **What types of knowledge/training do they want?**

The critical training/knowledge here is in Word and Excel. Because the advertisement does not specify a level of expertise, it is fair here to assume that you will need to be reasonably proficient in both. You will need to know what the programs do, how to produce standard documents in both packages, and how to print them out or otherwise present them. You might need to become very proficient in one or both of these packages.

Here is your chance to find out whether you are a Sherlock Holmes or an Inspector Clouseau. Now try examining some ads yourself. All you have to do is analyse three advertisements using our seven job advertisement interrogation questions. Use the approach we took in the last exercise as a framework, and try to be as concise as possible without missing out on anything important. You can then compare your answers with the experts' answers that follow. To make things a bit easier, we won't test you on Question 1 because there is no reason why you need to know the technical details of a job if you are not interested in it yourself. At the end, add up your scores to see how you did. Here is the first ad, and good luck!

exercise 2

Computer analyst/ programmer

An outstanding opportunity exists to join our leading edge Software Consultancy as an Analyst Programmer using the latest client/server technology. We are looking for creative and innovative thinkers who have a strong desire to be the best they can be in an environment that offers vast opportunities and rewards to dedicated and determined staff. You will be working and/or be trained alongside some of the best software developers in the field. Experience in Visual Basic, Access, SQL Server, and internet development with degree-level qualifications would be highly regarded. If you are ambitious and have an enthusiastic personality, you are ideal for these challenging and exciting roles.

My analysis is ...

1   Check terminology

_____

_____

_____

2   Type of industry/company

_____

_____

_____

Top salary and remuneration, bonuses and incentives, with UK and/or international travel opportunities on offer to the right applicant/s.

Send CV to:

Human Resources Director
Softly Softly Ltd
Lock Hill St
Sheffield, S. Yorks
SH21 9PT

3   Main purpose of the job

_____

_____

_____

4   Importance of the role to the company

_____

_____

_____

5   Skills required

_____

_____

_____

6   Personal qualities wanted

_____

_____

_____

7   Knowledge/training wanted

_____

_____

_____

exercise 2   The experts' analysis

1   Check terminology (not tested)

2   Type of industry/company

Software consultancy.

3   Main purpose of the job

Software development using client/server technology. In this case, you would probably have to liaise with clients and come up with solutions to their software problems. This would often involve writing special programs for the clients using the computer languages listed in the ad, such as Visual Basic or Access.

4   Importance of the role to the company

'Creative and innovative thinkers' – the company is looking for people who can think outside the box in developing new software products. In other words, you should be good at being able to write computer programs that can do the tasks required by the client. Your ability to deliver programs that not only work well but also address the client's needs is probably of central importance to the company.

5   Skills required

Ability to develop new software products using Visual Basic, Access, SQL Server and the internet.

6   Personal qualities wanted

Creative, innovative, ambitious, dedicated, determined (tenacious?), enthusiastic. All these personal qualities suggest somebody who is good at solving the problems that clients have. This may involve coming up with different solutions for every client rather than just trying to apply the same solution to every problem. This is the 'innovative' and 'creative' part. The need for dedication and determination suggests that you need to be able to see a problem through until it is solved and not give up too easily. 'Enthusiasm' probably suggests that they are looking for somebody who relishes problem-solving.

They want people who 'have a strong desire to be the best they can be'. What do they mean by this? It sounds like they want someone who is always pushing themselves to work harder, deliver more and keep learning. Perhaps this is because the technology is changing all the time. Perhaps it is because the clients are particularly demanding. Maybe it's because they have fewer analysts than necessary for the amount of work coming in.

7   Knowledge/training wanted

The knowledge and training required are reasonably clearly stated. You must be able to use the computer programs they mention to a high standard. Tertiary qualifications seem to be valued, too.

exercise 3

Sales representatives

Deci Co. in Glasgow requires Sales
Representatives to expand their sales to
corporate clients. While experience in the
printing industry is not essential, a proven
sales and service ability in the above market
would be a clear advantage. You should be
highly motivated and focused on building
a client base. You understand that success
comes from building relationships with
customers and tenaciously developing and
promoting printing solutions to a wide
industry client base. This position suits a
practical results-driven achiever who seeks an
attractive remuneration package.

Send CV to:

Douglas Giles
Giles Recruitment
PO Box 73
Glasgow
G73 2PU

My analysis is ...

1 **Check terminology**

_____

_____

_____

2 **Type of industry/company**

_____

_____

_____

3 **Main purpose of the job**

_____

_____

_____

4 **Importance of the role to the company**

_____

_____

_____

5 **Skills required**

_____

_____

_____

6 **Personal qualities wanted**

_____

_____

_____

7   Knowledge/training wanted

_____

_____

_____

exercise 3 The experts' analysis

1   **Check terminology (not tested)**

2   **Type of industry/company**

Deci Co. printing products and services. What services and products do they offer? How can you find out? Call the company for a brochure. Google them and see what classification the company is listed under. Do you have any friends who might have an idea – people working in the business, or even people who work near the company's address in Glasgow?

3   **Main purpose of the job**

Selling printing products and providing services to corporate clients. This probably will involve persuading clients to use your company to print all their brochures, stationery or whatever else the company offers.

What do they mean by 'expand sales to corporate clients'? They obviously want to sell their printing services to business customers. However, it is not completely clear whether they already sell to corporate customers and they want you to grow that existing business, or whether they currently only sell to the public and they want you to help them expand into a new market. Do they already have a list of corporate customers they wish to target or are they expecting you to generate leads from scratch?

4   **Importance of the role to the company**

Expanding sales via building and servicing a new client base. The sales position is a crucial one for many companies, because without clients there is no business.

5   **Skills required**

The sorts of skills required will include:

- selling skills – securing new clients
- customer service – looking after existing clients
- problem solving – identifying opportunities for new clients.

6   **Personal qualities wanted**

These will include: highly motivated, tenacious, results-driven and achievement-orientated. These skills are important because sales staff often are paid a high proportion of their salary as commission on the sales that they achieve. Consequently you need to be the type of person who will go looking for new opportunities (motivated), be prepared to bounce back quickly when a client says no initially (tenacious) and have a need to achieve goals or meet sales targets (achievement-orientated).

7   **Knowledge/training wanted**

Knowledge of the printing industry would be useful because it will mean you will understand the products, services and technology, know who your competitors are, who are the most likely good clients and so on. Knowledge of strategies to build a client base would also be extremely useful. This might be a good existing network of contacts who may turn into future clients, or experience of building up a network of clients in a previous job.

exercise 4

General manager – Technology

Our client, a national leading retailer, is seeking a General Manager to lead their business in a period of strong growth here in the UK and overseas.

My analysis is ...

1   **Check terminology**

_____

_____

_____

The role

Principally the role will focus on developing a strategic IT plan that supports business objectives and future system requirements. There is a need to review and evaluate existing hardware/software and to manage a small support team.

The person

You are a business manager first and foremost who understands the retail industry. You have a thorough understanding of information technology, including current and future directions. You possess strong people management skills and appreciate the importance of getting the best out of your staff. You have exceptional presentation skills and can tailor content to suit a broad audience. Excellent written presentation skills are required to communicate organisational needs and persuade senior management to implement system changes. This is an excellent opportunity for a successful individual to join a rapidly developing organisation and to make an impact on its future direction.

Send CV to:

Claudia Joy
Claudia Joy Ltd
PO Box 7
London WC1E 2PL

2   Type of industry/company

_____

_____

_____

3   Main purpose of the job

_____

_____

_____

4   Importance of the role to the company

_____

_____

_____

5   Skills required

_____

_____

_____

6   Personal qualities wanted

_____

_____

_____

7   Knowledge/training wanted

_____

_____

_____

exercise 4   The experts' analysis

1 **Check terminology (not tested)**

2 **Type of industry/company**

Leading national retailer: the company sells products to consumers (and possibly may manufacture them too).

3 **Main purpose of the job**

Managing the development and implementation of a strategic IT plan. Making sure the company has in place an IT system that can deal adequately with all the computing and communication needs of the company now and in the foreseeable future.

What are the 'business objectives' that your strategic IT plan will have to support? How large and how out of date is the existing infrastructure? Are they looking for an understanding of both company-facing and customer-facing technology?

4 **Importance of the role to the company**

Providing IT solutions that are aligned with current business needs and anticipated future IT requirements is very important. There are some sorry tales around about companies having to scrap their new computer systems because they found them to be inadequate to do the job required of them. Of course such blunders are not cheap to fix.

5 **Skills required**

The sorts of skills required are listed below:

- leadership – implementing change
- strategic business planning
- decision making
- people management – managing a small support team
- performance management – keeping the team's performance at the appropriate level
- presentation skills – oral and written.

6 **Personal qualities wanted**

A persuasive and decisive person probably would do well here. The emphasis is on being good at getting the rest of the team working effectively and being good at taking decisions. The last point may sound strange but managers who are unable to decide between one of several options can cause tremendous problems at work, because while they are prevaricating, nothing productive gets done!

7 **Knowledge/training wanted**

The sorts of skills that would be useful include:

- knowledge of the retail industry

- business management

- IT (internet, intranet, extranet)

- change management techniques.

How did you score?

Now you have analysed the sample ads, and compared your answers to those offered by our team of experts, you can find out how many points you've scored to assess how well you read the ads.

How did you score?

Now you have analysed the sample ads, and compared your answers to those offered by our team of experts, you can find out how many points you've scored to assess how well you read the ads.

Give yourself two points each time your answer agrees with the experts. Total up your score for each job ad and look up your score below.

Scoring

0–8 points Inspector Clouseau – yikes! Best to go back and start again. Writing a CV that addresses only a couple of key points is likely to get it thrown out with the rest. It may be the reason you've missed out being short-listed previously.

10–30 points Dr Watson – still some work to do but you're almost half-way there. What did you miss? Go back and check the sections you scored most poorly on.

32–42 points Sherlock Holmes – congratulations! The closer you scored to 42, the better chance you have of being short-listed. But be careful! In some cases, failing to identify the importance of some fundamentals like industry knowledge can still result in an almost perfect CV being rejected.

If at this stage you were unable to answer some of the questions clearly, then maybe it is because you need extra information. The following chapters describe some of the sources in more detail – so you know what you should be looking for.

CHAPTER 5

Job descriptions

ob descriptions are another very important source of information about a job. A job description is often provided when you contact a company asking for further details. Sometimes an employer will request that you phone to collect a job description before you apply for a job. Sometimes a job description will be on hand as part of the company's normal human resources documentation. In essence, it is a longer version of the job advertisement. Some job descriptions also go into greater detail about the company and its history. In analysing job descriptions, you should ask the same seven questions as you did with the job advertisement. Here is a sample job description.

▶ job description

General manager (project development)

The company (Winter, Earl & Bright (Web Ltd))

Winter, Bright & Earl (Web Ltd) provide integrated materials, handling and distribution services for a broad and diverse client base throughout the UK. They are active in the marketplace, identifying new opportunities and providing a broad range of solutions to a diverse group of potential new clients.

The General Manager (Project Development) will play a significant role in business development, as does the General Manager (Business Development). To meet ongoing growth and the demands of project management, Winter, Bright & Earl have created the role of General Manager (Project Development), a role planned to play an integral part in the ongoing upgrading and development of the Group.

The role

Winter, Earl & Bright are currently constructing a new facility in the North East. In the next 12 months, 4 sites are targeted for upgrade evaluation, with a further 16 sites across the UK targeted for evaluation of handling systems, with potential upgrades planned for 3 during that period. It is expected that the General Manager (Project Development) will bring exceptional Project Management, Logistics Management and Business Management skills to the Group and will be able to add value to the team, supporting the development of systems and solutions for targeted clients in the business development process, translating these into operational plans and taking into consideration all elements in the establishment of a new distribution centre from siting to construction, layout, systems, computer hardware and software, rolling stock, staffing levels, communication and administration.

The accountabilities of the role are as follows:

- identification of specific projects within existing operations, to prioritise resources in the formulation of action plans
- maintenance of project teams at required levels of skill to ensure projects are professionally managed
- establishment of detailed project plans specific to existing identified projects to manage the projects according to plan
- management of specific projects to identify project plans to ensure projects are delivered on time
- establishment of project plans for all new business projects and managing of projects in line with the plans to ensure new business is implemented with maximum customer satisfaction
- the development and fostering of client relationships in the implementation of projects to maximise customer satisfaction
- the establishment of projects in line with the Winter, Bright & Earl established standards of quality, excellence and provision of appropriate technological solutions.

The General Manager (Project Development) will become a member of a strong management executive, with the bulk of the team being in their early to mid-30s, reporting to a General Manager who, although having an open door policy, expects his general management to operate independently and liaise with him on a needs basis. With the establishment of Project Development as a key function within the organisation, the Group General Manager has planned a restructure of some areas of the operation, with three key provisionals being transferred to a new Project Development Team. It is expected that the new General Manager (Project Development) will be able to build and motivate this newly formed division to provide specialist support at all phases of the development chain.

Selection criteria

Experience

It is expected that the successful applicant will have Project Management experience and General Management experience and will have operated in a role at a similar level for a minimum of eight years. They will have moved into this role through a career in Mechanical/Civil Engineering or Project Management within the construction industry, transport industry, warehousing and logistics within a major fast-moving consumer goods organisation, retail, fast food, banking or petrochemicals. Importantly, the successful applicant will be able to lay claim to a track record of delivery of projects on time and within budget.

The position description highlights the skills needed in this role as knowledge and experience in strategic planning and analysis, as well as:

- project management skills
- leadership and communication skills
- financial analysis and management accounting skills
- understanding and experience of CSI (continuous service improvement)
- process reengineering and benchmarking
- operational management of the field of activity
- a grasp of the core business disciplines needed for operational success
- an understanding of the ER (Employee Relations) environment and the options and process available for enterprise bargaining
- basic familiarity with ER Policy
- understanding of Commercial Law as it relates to fixing contracts, entering leases and submitting tenders
- understanding of the broader regulatory environment as it affects occupational health, workers' compensation, taxation, management and public liability.

Educational background

The successful applicant will have tertiary qualifications in a business or engineering discipline.

Personal qualities

The successful applicant will possess the following qualities:

- strategic thinking
- consummate business judgement
- the ability to influence others
- relationship management skills
- team leadership skills
- excellent listening and communication skills
- initiative
- an achievement orientation.

In short, Winter, Earl & Bright expect an individual with innovation and vision, who can lead people effectively.

The successful applicant will have broad exposure to a diverse group of clients and suppliers and will be expected to operate effectively at all levels. It is expected that this individual will develop an awareness and knowledge of all elements affecting Winter, Bright & Earl's business operations and be able to add value to the total executive.

Employment conditions

Salary

A base salary will be negotiated in the vicinity of £44,000 per annum. Winter, Earl & Bright also offer significant incentive plans, with this position attracting a 21% bonus potential with 7% leveraged against personal contribution, 7% against project management and 7% against company results.

Other

A fully maintained car, a mobile phone and other standard benefits apply.

Searching for even more description

If a company is big enough, there may be information available in the media. This may be found in the business sections of papers, or on the internet. Sometimes companies will be in the papers for negative reasons such as industrial unrest, injuries or discrimination cases. While the media may give only a partial view of the company, you might get some really valuable information, too.

The internet is a particularly important source of information. Most companies now have home pages on the Web that will tell you a lot about them.

Company home pages can be searched for on the Web using standard search engines such as Google, Bing, Yahoo! and Excite. When searching, try a variety of key words such as 'BT' or 'Telecommunications Companies'. In Part 4, we provide a list of useful job-related links.

Many large-scale companies decide to sub-contract their recruiting to specialist management consulting firms such as PricewaterhouseCoopers, Accenture, and Saville and Holdsworth (SHL). These firms all have home pages and within their pages there may well be links to their clients' home pages. Try looking on the webpages of the companies that place recruitment advertisements (such as Jobsite and Monster). The internet is also becoming an increasingly popular medium to advertise jobs, and for people to submit their CVs. More information on using the internet can be found in Part 4 of this book.

Finally, there are always people out there happy to pass on their opinions with little regard to how accurate they may be. We've all met the sort: 'Oh, I wouldn't work for them, they want your soul', or 'You know they invest in military hardware', or 'The boss is a drunk – it's well known', or 'They sell cigarettes to children'. Try to get as much objective evidence as possible about prospective employers. If people pass on these sorts of comments, ask them to justify what they say, or where they heard it. If they cannot come up with anything more credible than 'everyone knows that!', or 'a friend of my brother', we suggest you disregard it.

They must want Superman!

Having read all these ads and job descriptions, you could be forgiven for thinking that companies are looking for extraordinary skills and abilities in their employees. It is only human nature – after all, if you were the employer, wouldn't you be looking for the best possible employees? However, do not be put off by the over-the-top language often used. Behind all of the bluster you have probably got all the qualities they are looking for.

brilliant tip

Job ads often sound as though they are looking for a superhuman candidate! Don't be too easily put off from applying. If you are not in the game, you cannot win it.

Remember that your aim, as a job detective analysing job advertisements, is to try to work out what the ideal candidate or 'prime suspect' might look like. If the person you come up with could not possibly exist (no one is that perfect!) you have probably gone wrong somewhere. Go back and see where you might have exaggerated the required attributes, or where the employer might be being unrealistic.

One of the requirements that tends to put people off applying for a job is a demand for vast amounts of experience. If you think about it for a moment you will realise that just having experience in a role does not guarantee that you will be good at that job. What employers really want when they ask for experience are the benefits someone good will have gained from high quality experience. If you identify these potential benefits, you may be able to fit yourself to the role even if you don't have exactly the experience they are asking for. Below are some areas in which the benefits of experience may show.

Skills and abilities

- What would someone with good experience be able to do better than someone with poor experience?
- What mistakes would someone with poor experience make that someone with good experience would avoid?

Knowledge, understanding and awareness

- What would someone with good experience know already that someone with poor experience might have to discover?
- What would someone with good experience learn more quickly than someone with poor experience?
- What would someone with good experience notice that someone with poor experience might miss?

Credibility and marketability

- How would someone with good experience be better able to establish necessary credibility with key stakeholders than someone with poor experience?
- What added value to potential stakeholders or customers would someone with good experience provide over someone with poor experience?

Track record and reliability

- What levels of achievement are more likely from someone with good experience?
- What kind of challenging situations would someone with good experience have dealt with that someone with poor experience might not have?
- In what ways would someone with good experience have proved themselves more effectively than someone with poor experience?

Efficiency and prioritisation

- What activities would a candidate with good experience perform more quickly than someone with poor experience?
- What wasteful or unnecessary practices would someone with good experience have eliminated?

When you have answered all these questions, you should have a much clearer picture of what it is that the company wants. It is now that you can form your plan of attack.

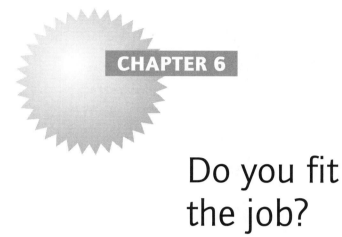

CHAPTER 6

Do you fit the job?

Applying for a job can be very competitive, especially if the company has a good reputation, or the position is particularly exciting – both things you are looking for in a new job. It doesn't pay to overestimate your skills beyond your abilities, but it seriously disadvantages you if you are overly negative. It constantly amazes recruiters when they receive, all too commonly, covering letters that begin: 'Dear Sir, First of all can I point out that I don't have the required experience, but …'

Of course, nobody likes to appear big-headed, and it can be hard to describe your own abilities and not feel this way.

You see it's awfully hard to talk or write about your own stuff because if it is any good you yourself know about how good it is – but if you say so yourself you feel like a shit.

Ernest Hemingway

The point is that a potential employer wants to know what you can do, and playing down genuine abilities will not present you in the proper light.

Who are you?

Now you've painted the picture of the ideal candidate in the previous chapters, how do you go about listing your skills? Here are some pointers to help you describe yourself.

When it comes to describing themselves, many people forget potentially vital details, or think that some achievements are probably irrelevant to their

CV. Then again, there are some people who play down their achievements. Finally, there are those people who just cannot see that 'played in the under-sevens soccer team' is not as important as 'was elected as Prime Minister'.

In our research we found that those candidate CVs that were focused on outcomes and achievements were more likely to be short-listed by recruiters than CVs that described the duties and responsibilities of each previous job (see Figure 6.1).

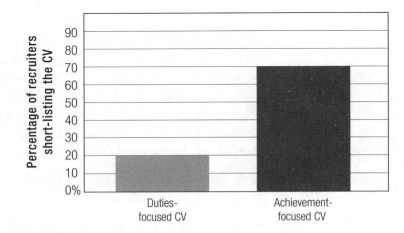

Figure 6.1 What is the most successful focus for the CV?

The four most common faults here are:

1 forgetting some potentially impressive achievements
2 thinking some achievements are not relevant
3 playing down your achievements
4 including every boring, irrelevant detail.

You will be saying to yourself, 'Hang on, they are telling me not to exclude relevant stuff and in the next breath they are saying do not include irrelevant material. That's really helpful!'

We will introduce you to some exercises that will assist you in determining what is important and what is not.

First of all you need a list of your past activities and your achievements. We suggest that to ensure you do not omit anything by accident, you should try to list your past in as much detail as possible. At this stage do not attempt to decide whether the information is relevant or not.

We have developed some forms to help you get all the relevant details down in some order. Some people may find it easier to jot things down as they come to them which is just fine. But you may wish to put all the information onto our templates when you have finished.

Building a personal history

Divide your life into the following sections where applicable:

Stage of life	Use this template
Secondary school (typically 11–16 or 18 years old)	Template 1
Vocational training (16–22 years old)	Template 1
University (usually 18–21 years old)	Template 1
Any postgraduate training (typically in your 20s)	Template 1
Jobs held in the first 5 years after completing your training/ education (between 20 and 30 years)	Template 2
Jobs held in your 30s	Template 2
Jobs held in your 40s	Template 2
Jobs held in your 50s and so on	Template 2
Life achievements/awards/community work/sports and hobbies	Template 3

Of course, many career histories will vary from the one shown. Here are a couple of other models.

For people without formal qualifications:

- jobs held between 15 and 20
- jobs held 20–30

- jobs held 30–40
- jobs held 40–50 and later

you should use Templates 2 and 3.

For people who joined the workforce later in life:

- what you did before starting training/joining the workforce
- any training
- first 5 years of work
- next 10 years
- the next 10 years, and so on

you should use all three templates, but it may be that Template 3 (the Life template) could be the most important.

You can see the general pattern that we are suggesting is to divide up your life into sections that you might think of as:

- early work and training
- early jobs post-training
- mid-career jobs
- later career jobs.

When you have settled on a way of dividing up your life that suits you, use our templates to guide the process.

On Template 1 try to list the following:

- any training you undertook
- the institution
- everything you studied (the correct titles of the subjects)
- the results you achieved in each subject
- the overall result
- show that training was/could be useful to you in your work.

Template 1: Training template

For each place you did any training, complete the following details.

Secondary/ Tertiary	St Custards University	Dates attended	From 2006	To 2009
Subjects studied	Results	Teams or clubs	Achievements	
Latin	C	Basketball	I played in the cup-winning club team in 2006. I captained the team in 2008 and we came second out of 20 teams	
Home Economics	A			
Sports	D			
English	B			
Maths	C			
Spanish	U			
Geography	D			

Template 2: Jobs template

Employer Name and Address	Old Joe Pigtail And Associates 2 Railway Cuttings East Cheam Trumpton-On-Peas	Dates attended	From 2010	To 2011
Reason for leaving		To get broader experience with Mega Media International		
Job title	Dates	Key duties	Achievements/promotions	
Junior Accounts Consultant	2010–11	Assisting Accounts Consultant	Analysing sales figures I was the first employee to be promoted to Accounts Consultant within one year, and also the youngest person to have held that position in the company's history	

Accounts Consultant	2011–12	Preparing client monthly reports on sales and promotions activities	I redesigned the client reports to provide a clearer picture of year-on-year progress

Training undertaken	Instructor/ organisation	Date 2012	Description	What I learned
Effective Management	Lars Toeplast Peak Managers Blue Mountains		Wilderness course on teamwork and delegation	Taught me to set clear goals and listen to others in a group

Template 3: Life template

Activity	Dates	Description	Achievements/ personal development	Possible relevance to job
Community work and volunteering	2011 to date	Being a young leader in local Scout pack	Satisfaction of giving something back to local community	Shows energy to use my skills outside of normal areas
Hobbies/ interests	2012 to date	Playing the oboe in the heavy woodwind band 'The Welsh Springer Spaniels'	Won the band's 'Eisteddfod the Men of Harlech/ Delilah' medley	Requires discipline, commitment and stoicism in face of oboe jokes
Sports	2004 to date	Basketball, at school, and now for the college 1st team	Social life, helps keep me fit	Helps me be a team player Reduces stress
Other	2010	On the organising committee of the Festival of Food, a two-week festival aimed at promoting the local restaurants and raising awareness about diet		Good organisational skills

It is worth mentioning here that one of the most frequent difficulties for people reading CVs is to work out what exactly a particular qualification or result actually means. Have a look at what we have to say about this in Chapter 8.

On Template 2 list:

- all the jobs you have held
- the name of the companies
- the title of your job
- your responsibilities
- your reason for leaving
- your achievements (which we will discuss in more detail)
- any promotions.

On Template 3 include any extracurricular activities:

- sports
- committees
- interest groups (for example, amateur drama)
- training courses (such as wine appreciation, motor mechanics)
- charitable work
- hobbies.

The following tip may seem a little harsh, but remember this is from the horse's mouth!

brilliant tip

Do a lot with your life so that there is good, interesting material to include in a well-presented CV!

Employers talk a lot about their employees 'making a contribution' and if you can demonstrate this in your CV you will be a more attractive candidate. The more time you spend away from passive activities like watching the television, the more likely it is that you will have positive things to say on your CV. Think for one minute how society views people who do nothing but watch television in their leisure time – they are called 'couch potatoes', or worse, and this is especially damning for younger people.

List your achievements for each part of your life

It is surprising how quickly some people can forget what they have achieved or play down their role in successes. Sometimes this is because you are not feeling too good about yourself. You may have lost your job, been unemployed for a long time, or you have been out of the workforce for a long time. You must learn to recognise the symptoms if you are playing down your achievements. It is amazing, but we have seen countless university graduates who hold excellent degrees and Masters or PhD degrees who say, 'But I haven't really achieved anything ...'

Look closely at all the activities you have listed in each period of your life.

Now think really carefully about anything that you might have achieved during this time. It might be useful for you to dip into Chapter 8 now and have a look at our 'Gestalt rule of proximity'. It states that people will credit you with an achievement if you were sufficiently close to it. For example, if you were a member of a team that saw sales increase 20 per cent annually, you should claim it as an achievement, even if you can't say for sure exactly how much of that outcome was directly related to your efforts.

Breaking through the modesty barrier

Figure 6.2 shows the modesty barrier. Imagine yourself at the centre of the diagram. The first thick-lined circle is your view of how good you think you are. Social pressure to be modest keeps our self-image firmly in check. However, you can see that, for most of us, this is a self-limiting view of how good we really are. Our true potential is the outermost circle. Between them is the modesty barrier dotted line. Most of us can be persuaded to improve our view of ourselves, but we tend to reach a modesty barrier at which point we feel really uncomfortable with the self-promotion. Your job

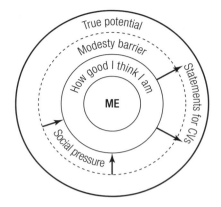

Figure 6.2 Breaking through the modesty barrier

is to break through the modesty barrier to write positive things on your CV. Notice that, even though you may be uncomfortable with the results, your claims still will be safely within your true potential. Occasionally some people make claims beyond their true potential, but don't you worry about doing that – it tends to be only politicians who indulge in such behaviour!

Achievements and facts – a balancing act

If you look at our templates, you will see that they are divided roughly down the middle. On the left-hand side are the dates and jobs and hobbies. On the right-hand side we have the achievements, the promotions, the personal development.

brilliant tip

Strike a balance on the information side.

It is our experience that people are great at loading the left-hand side of the see-saw (see Figure 6.3) while tending to forget the right-hand side. Why is this?

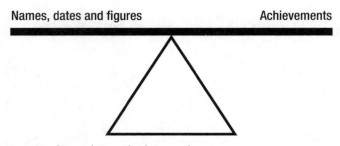

Figure 6.3 A general template – the 'see-saw'

Some reasons why people focus on 'names, dates and figures' are:

- they are easier to remember
- people are taught to be modest
- names, dates and figures are easier to confirm
- some people get lazy, letting the names and dates speak for them
- writing them out doesn't take much thinking.

We believe very strongly that achievements are extremely important. You can see from Figure 6.3 that excluding achievements will lead to an unbalanced CV. This leads us to the next two golden rules:

1 CVs exist to tell the world what you have achieved. Achievements count.

2 Everybody has achievements, some are just better at hiding them than others.

Here are some examples to help you. Check our list of possible achievements:

- promotions
- increasing sales figures
- running a project to change something in your company
- being part of a team that … (what did your team do?)
- winning an award or prize (no matter how trivial, list it)
- good results in exams or assessments
- gaining qualifications (like a degree, advanced driving qualification, heavy goods vehicle licence)
- employee of the month award

- customer service/quality awards
- outside work achievements – raising money for charity, being elected to a committee
- winning a league, a race, captaining a sports team
- long periods without absence from work (such as no sick days in three years)

brilliant tip

Keeping your CV up to date is essential because you never know when you might need to apply for a new job. Jim Bright and Robert Pryor have developed a chaos theory of career development. Part of the theory is that people choose jobs on the basis of chance or unplanned events. They found that 70 per cent of a large sample of people said their careers had been significantly influenced by a chance event. Organisational psychologist Lucy Harpham and Jim Bright followed this up and replicated the finding – the majority of people will have their careers influenced by a chance event[1]. So you never know when you'll need your CV in a hurry!

- running a marathon or a fun run
- helping to paint a school/community centre
- implementation or design of systems or processes
- improving efficiencies or overhauling processes.

At the end of this chapter you should have three completed templates, and they should look well-balanced. That is, both the right and left sides of them should have plenty of information.

Well done! You now have most of the ingredients you require to build a top CV. Before we do that, in the next chapter we will consider the final ingredient – you!

---

[1] Bright, J.E.H., Pryor, R.G.L. and Harpham, L. (2005). The role of chance events in career decision making. *Journal of Vocational Behavior*. 66 (3), 561–576.

CHAPTER 7

What sort of person are you?

et's face it, work takes up a major part of our time, so it stands to reason that people want to work with colleagues who are pleasant and easy to get along with. If you had to choose between two equally talented workmates – one whom you hated, and the other whom you liked – would there really be any decision to make? Increasingly companies are becoming aware that their employees' personal habits and their work personality can not only influence the harmony of the workforce but may also directly influence the quality of the work done too.

Many job ads these days list the personal qualities companies believe are important to be successful in their organisations. Many companies take this information very seriously and some will use quite sophisticated psychological tests to measure your ability to work in teams, or how quickly you might lose your temper. Other companies will invite you to join a group of other applicants to assess how well you interact with others.

Generally this sort of information is collected after reading your CV – in interviews and so on – but it is a good idea to emphasise in your CV that you will fit the company's desired 'personality'.

In this chapter, we highlight some of the most common 'psychological' traits that employers look for, explain what they mean, and demonstrate how to emphasise your strengths in these areas.

What are the most common qualities employers look for?

From a consideration of job advertisements, the following is our list of the eight most popular qualities desired:

1 Communication skills, verbal and written
2 Team skills/team player
3 Attention to detail
4 Energy/dynamism/drive
5 Initiative
6 Ability to handle pressure
7 Enthusiasm
8 Leadership.

What do employers want when they ask for these qualities?

In order to understand what employers look for when they ask for these competencies, it can be helpful to work out what actions and behaviours you would observe in someone who was demonstrating high levels of these qualities. Many recruiters do exactly that when they assess your suitability and potential. They use something called a competency framework which gives examples of the actions and behaviours to look out for in a candidate's CV and in their answers to interview questions.

Many organisations, especially in the public sector, make their competency frameworks available to candidates in order to help them prepare. You should make sure that you have read and understood these if they are available. Even if the organisation you are applying to hasn't produced a framework, you would benefit from looking at ones that are available because many of the behaviours are appropriate to a range of jobs. Just make sure that you also think about how these competencies might be used to achieve the specific goals of the role you are applying for.

Communication skills, verbal and written

An excellent communicator would:

- Listen carefully and show that they were listening through non-verbal communication and paraphrasing
- Ask appropriate questions to gather information and check their understanding
- Find out what the other person already knows to avoid giving them redundant information
- Decide on the most effective communication method in order to achieve their goals in particular circumstances
- Provide a clear and meaningful structure to their communications in order to aid understanding
- Anticipate potential misunderstandings and adjust their communication accordingly
- Observe and obtain feedback from others to ensure that the message has been received
- Refine and adapt their communication style to suit different audiences and conditions
- Take time to check the fluency and accuracy of what they say or write before communicating.

brilliant tip

Assume that communication skills are important for every job and try to demonstrate them in your CV.

Team skills/team player

An excellent team player would:

- Identify valuable team goals and needs, prioritise them above personal goals and needs, and promote them to other team members

- Maintain awareness of the motivation and mood of the team as a whole and of individual team members
- Strive to understand the strengths, styles and perspectives of other team members
- Support and encourage other team members when they need it
- Offer positive contributions and value the contributions of others
- Promote the achievements and talents of other team members as much as their own
- Seek to understand how their own work impacts on the effectiveness of other team members
- Fulfil their commitments to others who depend on their input
- Constructively address conflict and misunderstandings within the team.

Attention to detail

Someone with excellent attention to detail would:

- Show an understanding of the impact of inaccuracy and faults on the success of the wider business
- Explore the quality needs of the people who will be working with their output
- Decide on an appropriate level of accuracy balanced against the time constraints
- Allow time for quality checks when planning tasks
- Design systematic procedures to reduce the likelihood of mistakes
- Uncover the causes of errors to ensure that they do not happen again.

brilliant tip

Make sure there are no spelling mistakes. Use the spellchecker. Ensure your grammar and punctuation are correct.

▶ brilliant example

One recent example of a CV we saw from a student read: 'I have excellent attention to deatail'! Not only does this sentence undermine itself, it sends out warning signs – what other weaknesses does this candidate have?

Energy/dynamism/drive/enthusiasm

A dynamic person would:

- Adopt a positive attitude to all tasks no matter how challenging or unpleasant
- Volunteer for extra responsibility
- Set demanding but achievable goals for themselves and others
- Respond constructively to criticisms, seeking to improve for the future
- Seek feedback from others on how to become more effective
- Persist in the face of obstacles
- Recover quickly from setbacks and not dwell unproductively on past failures
- Encourage and motivate other people.

Initiative

Someone with excellent initiative would:

- Look for potential gains and opportunities in any situation
- Identify helpful contributions they could make without waiting to be told
- Seek to understand and anticipate the needs of others
- Have ideas for new and improved activities and make constructive suggestions
- Find solutions to problems rather than waiting for someone else to sort things out
- Take responsibility for their own learning in order to meet future challenges.

Ability to handle pressure

Someone who is excellent at handling pressure would:

- Anticipate the conditions that could make a task or situation stressful
- Prepare adaptable plans to address demands
- Take a step back from immediate activities to identify wider goals and priorities
- Prioritise conflicting tasks according to their impact on business needs
- Put in place systems and procedures to ensure routine tasks do not take time and energy from more important activities
- Monitor and control their own emotions and stress levels so that they maintain equilibrium
- Respond constructively to the emotions of others under stress and calmly enable them to focus on what is important.

Leadership

An excellent leader would:

- Seek information that would help them to understand the context for their actions
- Identify and communicate a clear vision for the team or organisation
- Seek input from followers and make decisions about a course of action
- Assess the abilities, motivations and working styles of their followers in order to appropriately allocate responsibilities
- Provide clear briefings to followers on their goals and tasks and check their understanding
- Monitor the performance and attitudes of followers and provide appropriate feedback and encouragement
- Take responsibility for the successes and failures of their team
- Treat everyone with impartiality, integrity and transparency.

How do you rate against the list of important skills?

Here are a few questions that might help you think about these skills in relation to yourself. Use these questions to trigger ideas about your personal qualities.

- Do you tend to get details right more often than not, or do you find details irritating?
- Do you prefer working in a team of people, or on your own?
- Do you like to be a leader, or a team member?
- Are you punctual for work?
- Would you say you are outgoing, like meeting people and going to parties, or do you prefer your own company, or just a few trusted friends?
- Do you tend to be cheerful and positive, or do you easily get depressed?
- When people make a lot of demands on you, do you tend to remain calm, or do you find yourself losing your temper?

All of the above questions are commonly asked of candidates by employers because they are regarded as important qualities in successful employees. You may be thinking that to any or all of those questions your answer is 'Sometimes yes, sometimes no', or 'It depends', or 'It is not as simple as that'. That is a perfectly reasonable response. The point is, if these are the qualities sought by employers, the more you can demonstrate them through deeds, the better.

Exercising your skills

The following exercises should help you address these 'personality requirements' of employers more easily.

Communication skills

List the people or group of people you commonly communicate with. Next to each person or group of people write down how you communicate. Is it face-to-face, in writing, or on the phone? What is your presentation style? Then write down how you know that what you're communicating has been successful. Take a look at our example, then try to fill out the table yourself.

exercise 1

WHO	WHAT	SUCCESS?
Managing director	Face-to-face question	Body language, no additional clarification needed
Unit leader	Presentation of monthly reports	Performance appraisal requested to coach others

Teamwork and leadership

List examples of your ability to get on well with co-workers. Here are some to guide you:

● 'The restructure motivated my new team, and we all took on extra duties to ensure that we accomplished our goals, which we actually exceeded every month.'

● 'Five of us were assigned to investigate why our customer service ratings were down. We divided the tasks up into different product areas, and decided on weekly team meetings. We soon discovered that there were some common problems, and our recommendations when implemented proved very popular.'

● 'I took on a departed colleague's duties to ensure a smooth service before a replacement was recruited for our team.'

● 'I was voted most popular team member twice last year.'

Remember, many jobs will be fairly clear whether they want a leader or a team member (or both). Looking like a leader when a team member is called for will have recruiters thinking this person will not take direction and will question decisions. Equally, if a leader is required, looking too much like 'one of the boys' might be interpreted as being a poor leader.

The following are some sample statements showing leadership:

- 'I reorganised the way payments were processed. This involved reassigning several staff, some job enlargement and the redundancy of three staff members.'
- 'Under my management, the group has shown record profits in the past eight quarters.'

Statements showing team membership are similar to those suggesting good relations with colleagues.

Try writing your own statements to show you are outgoing, like meeting people, going to parties, or that you prefer your own company or that of just a few trusted friends. Our examples follow:

- 'I enjoy public speaking.'
- 'I am the staff social representative.'
- 'I enjoy dealing with my customers.'
- 'I enjoyed my five years in sales.'

There are few jobs that would openly seek people who are not outgoing, but they do exist. Any job where contact with other employees or the public is not frequent would be a case in point. Such jobs include machine operators, back-room processing jobs or jobs where people are out 'on the road' alone like truck drivers, or people working from home. Inadvertent statements that may make you look a little anti-social would be:

- 'I have learned to be very self-reliant.'
- 'I worked in sole practice for 20 years.'
- 'I enjoy the challenge of myself against the elements on orienteering holidays.'

Attention to detail

List work tasks or preferably results where your attention to detail has been demonstrated. For example:

- 'I have never had documents I have typed sent back to me with factual or grammatical errors in them.'
- 'During my time in this post, I reduced the amount of internal mail that was incorrectly addressed by more than 30 per cent.'

Energy, enthusiasm and initiative

Try writing your own statements after reading these samples:

- 'I identified more effective procedures in the Accounts department, leading to increased productivity and customer satisfaction. Mustering the talent of our Finance department, I solicited employee ideas and persuaded Management to award the best idea a £500 incentive. These ideas resulted in savings of over £500,000 to the company.'

- 'I took on responsibility for reorganising client files to better improve storage and retrieval. Although this was an area in which I had limited experience, I contacted my colleagues in other parts of the company and by sharing ideas with them and working long hours I implemented a new system within two weeks (three weeks earlier than my manager had expected).'

Pressure

Statements that show your calm temperament, or ability to handle pressure, might look like this:

- 'My current role regularly involves having to produce briefing reports at extremely short notice. It is satisfying to get the job done against apparently impossible odds.'

- 'A key skill is to calm down angry passengers whose flights have been delayed.'

If there was a time when a job had to be finished by a deadline and you worked overnight or over the weekend to complete it, then write down the details next to the relevant job on your life history.

Finally, reflect on the places you have worked, the times you have worked (such as nightshifts or overtime) and teams you have worked with. Are there any things that stand out as particularly good or bad?

Where wouldn't you work?

Now is the time to make a list of things you will not put up with in the workplace. To do this, make three lists with the following headings:

1 I will never work in a place that. . .

2 I will only put up with … if it happens very rarely.

3 I would prefer not to work in a place that … but I know I can cope if necessary.

The things you might put on this list include:

- bad-tempered boss
- few people of my gender or ethnic background at work
- premises in the middle of town
- premises out of town
- no car parking
- very poor safety.

Your pantry of ingredients

You should now have several templates setting out all the things that you have done over your working life, and how you see yourself. Think of this as your 'pantry' of ingredients. This is what we will use to make your tailored CV, and brings us to our next brilliant tip.

brilliant tip

Take time every couple of months to update your skills and achievements list. This way you will always have an up-to-date list and you are less likely to forget your achievements over time.

Now you have all this information about yourself, you have one task left. Give all the information to somebody who knows you very well, and who you trust. Ask them, 'Is this me?' and 'Is there anything I've left out?' If you are embarrassed about showing someone else all those immodest achievements we asked you to list, blame us! We told you to do it.

You are now ready to start deciding what goes into your CV.

Before choosing a style of CV, you need to start matching your personal achievements and qualities with the job detective work you have done. You should, by this stage, have a good idea of what the job requirements are and this information should guide you in choosing which achievements and personal qualities you should include. The challenge here is different for different groups. Use our work history achievement chart below to assist you in this task.

Career stage	Information to emphasise	Key challenges for your CV
School leaver	Qualifications Personality/life skills Community involvement Any work experience Your age (so people do not expect too much work experience if you are young) Hobbies	Demonstrate to an employer that you have some skills to offer (either through your qualifications or through community involvement). Demonstrate readiness to enter the workforce through responsibility, reliability and maturity.
Graduate	Qualifications Any work experience, including visits and placements as a part of your studies Awards Community involvement Personality/life skills	Show an employer that you are more than just a brainbox, that you are well rounded, are involved in things outside study, that you have not wasted the opportunities that university offers. Demonstrate evidence of responsibility, leadership, maturity and, if relevant, commercial awareness.
Early career	Qualifications Work experience Work achievements Personality Life skills	Show how you have progressed and what new skills you've learned in the workforce. Show a logical pattern in the work history that tells a story, and that this job is the logical next step.
Mid-career	Work experience, especially the past five years, and anything relevant to the position applied for Work achievements Positions of leadership/responsibility Relevant training courses, or industry qualifications change Membership of professional associations	Demonstrate a period of sustained success and recognition at work. The story needs to tell of a steady (or faster) rise up the organisational ladder or, alternatively, a steady (or better) stream of achievement and recognition. Show a broadening of your industry experience, or mastery of your chosen skill.

Career stage	Information to emphasise	Key challenges for your CV
Late career	Leadership and management skills or mastery of a set of skills Wide experience across situations, organisations and/or countries Professional recognition of your status	Show that you can fit into the organisation and help them out from day one. Demonstrate a track record of success. Come across as totally sound and remove any doubts about your ability to do the job with assurance.
Career change	Transferable skills, any skills or experience that may be relevant to the chosen career Any relevant skills acquired in a previous career to the one you are leaving Evidence of personal qualities such as flexibility and willingness to learn	Think about your current work experience from an outsider's perspective. Can you portray mundane skills in a new light that makes them seem relevant? Convince the recruiter that this is a considered move and a logical progression, or sensible change. Minimise the differences between you and the new job.
Re-entry to the workforce after a break	Qualifications that are still current Any activities and achievements in the time away from work Efforts to keep yourself up to date, current market knowledge Personal qualities that are relevant to the job and that show market/commercial awareness	Show that you are not completely out of touch and that you have something very valuable to offer that ideally will not cost the company a lot of time and money in developing. Demonstrate how you spent your time out of the workforce responsibly and productively. Be aware that your reasons for being out of the workforce may not be highly valued by the employer.

CHAPTER 8

Making the
perfect fit

How do I set out my CV?

There are several ways of writing a CV. Different approaches work for different people. The three most popular CV styles are the:

1 chronological CV

2 functional CV

3 hybrid CV.

Chronological CV

This CV is the style many people use without thinking. It lists your training and jobs in order of the dates you commenced each of them. Typically, people list their most recent training or jobs first and proceed back to the first things they did. This is called the 'reverse chronological' CV.

The components of this CV are, in order:

1 Personal details.

2 Qualifications.

3 Professional development/training courses.

4 Employment history, including:
   - employer
   - dates of employment
   - positions held
   - achievements.

Here is a quick example of the chronological CV.

Bob Brown

Address: 10 Elm Ave
                        London, SW2 4UL

Contact details: (H) 020 8311 3111
                        (W) 020 8222 2222

Employment history

Jones Bros Ltd

Jones Bros is a large national company that owns a range of goods transportation systems. Next Day Freight provides distribution systems for a broad customer base including a range of major UK companies.

Regional Manager for Next Day Freight   3/10 to present

Reporting to the General Manager.

My major responsibilities in this position include acting as a change agent reshaping the business into a professional and profitable organisation with a strong emphasis on customer service. The bottom line responsibility of this position is a £50 million business unit employing 350 people in Sales, Administration, Operations, Marketing, Customer Service, Quality and Security.

My major achievements in this position include:

- creation and implementation of a regional business plan addressing major shortfalls in the business
- a successful merger with a £10 million business unit
- restructuring of the entire sales force
- negotiation and implementation of a new enterprise agreement
- complete management restructure
- introduction of new Management Information Systems
- negotiating the outsourcing of £2.5 million p.a. of casual labour
- coordinating the building of a major new depot facility
- implementation of a quantifiable quality improvement programme
- development of a new marketing strategy
- development of a major strategic industrial relations plan to create greater incentive for the workforce
- leading the business unit to its best profit performance.

National Petroleum Ltd

National is a major petroleum company that owns refineries nationally, as well as having a major franchise network of petrol stations.

National Distribution Network Manager   3/05 to 2/10

Reporting to the National Planning Manager.

In this role, I was responsible for the strategic development and network rationalisation of the wholesale distribution business worth over £80 million p.a. to company profit. I was responsible for maintaining primary trade and developing an environment for improved profit performance based on best practices, operating efficiency and optimum capital investment.

Major milestones in this role included:

- comprehensive review of the sector and development of an integrated business plan for the next century
- development of a new network process to contain the best demographic mix of distribution and marketing
- development and implementation of a merchandising-based franchise package
- implementation of a business planning process for independent distributors
- strategic business review of a £300 million subsidiary
- management of the wholesale investment budget to achieve corporate objectives
- successful rationalisation and restructuring of the distributor business to improve the return on investment.

Regional Finance Manager   3/03 to 2/05

Reporting to the Regional Manager.

My major responsibilities in this role were the financial performance of the dealer and distributor businesses within the area, and entailed the management of profitability, franchisee selection and administration.

Senior Reseller Area Manager   1/01 to 2/03

Reporting to the Wholesale Network Development Manager.

Responsible for bottom-line profit, achievement of volume targets, financial management and credit control, tendering for new business and network development.

Marketing, Planning and Economics Officer   2/99 to 12/00
Responsible for SWOT analyses, forecasting and preparation of cost submissions.

Transport Distribution Manager   2/98 to 1/99
Consulting to wholesale fuel distributors.

Rundle and Smith Chartered Accountants   *1/96 to 1/98*

Team audit work for a range of companies.
Reason for leaving: to pursue a marketing career.

Qualifications

1993–1995   BA in Management, University of London
Majoring in Accounting and Commercial Law

Professional development

I have attended training courses in the following:

- Consultative selling
- Analytical skills
- Negotiation
- Time management
- Business management
- Executive development programme.

Interests

Swimming, tennis and bike riding, competitive squash, share dealing.

Referees

Available upon request.

Functional CV

This is a style that emphasises the skills of the individual and their achievements. It is often used when the applicant lacks formal qualifications, or their qualifications are judged obsolete or irrelevant. If you have had many different jobs with no clear pattern of progression, or a lot of gaps in your work history, some people recommend this approach. You do not, after all, want to present your career as a drunken stagger through the world of work!

Bob Brown

Address:	10 Elm Ave
	London, SW2 4UL
Contact details:	(H) 020 8311 3111
	(W) 020 8222 2222

Skills, knowledge, attributes and abilities

Communication skills

In my role as Regional Manager for Next Day Freight I am required to liaise across a broad cross-section of employees. In order to keep employees abreast of company direction and anticipated changes, I implemented briefing sessions held across all shifts once a month. Here I was able to communicate directly with the staff myself and field any questions. Employee satisfaction regarding communication improved from 2.5 to 4.3 over a 12-month period.

Business management

I have a sound knowledge of business management principles. Having completed studies in Management at the University of London, I have continued to keep myself up to date with recent trends and developments by subscribing to journals and magazines. I have also attended several training courses, including the London Business School Executive Development Programme and specialist management courses. Over the past three years, I have implemented ideas gained from my knowledge to restructure our sales force, and supervise the implementation of a new Management Information System and quality improvement programme.

Selling skills

As National Distribution Network Manager for National Petroleum Ltd, I was responsible for developing a merchandising-based franchise package which aimed at converting successful franchisees with other companies to National Petroleum. I developed a programme that targeted the top 100 successful franchisees and, by interviewing a cross-section, identified reasons most would convert. I then developed a selling kit for representatives to use and conducted selling-skills training courses for representatives to develop better levels of skill. I dealt with the top three clients personally and all three converted. Of the remaining 97 franchisees, 70 per cent converted.

Negotiation skills

In my capacity as Regional Manager for Next Day Freight, I have been required to address numerous issues regarding workforce planning. This has included outsourcing £2.5 million worth of casual labour, implementing a staff incentive programme and developing a new enterprise agreement. These represented major changes for our existing and often volatile workforce. By developing a committee (which I chaired) involving employee, management and union representatives, we have been able to successfully introduce the required changes without any lost time. Employee satisfaction with working conditions has risen from 1.8 to 4.0 over the past three years.

Tenacity

On my appointment to the position of Regional Manager Next Day Freight, I quickly identified potential cost savings in merging our business unit with our sister company's (Parcel Pick Up) business unit worth £10 million. The project to merge the two units was finally realised last month after planning and negotiations spanning more than three years. Anticipated cost savings as a result of the merger are likely to be in the vicinity of £5 billion.

Summary of employment history

3/10 to now	Jones Bros Ltd	Regional Manager Next Day Freight
3/05 to 2/10	National Petroleum Ltd	National Distribution Network Manager
3/03 to 2/05		Regional Finance Manager
1/01 to 2/03		Senior Reseller Area Manager
2/99 to 12/00		Marketing, Planning and Economics Officer
2/98 to 1/99		Transport Distribution Manager
1/96 to 1/98	Rundle and Smith Chartered Accountants	Team audit work for a range of companies. Reason for leaving: to pursue a marketing career.

Qualifications

1993–1995   BA in Management, University of London
Majoring in Accounting and Commercial Law

Interests

Swimming, tennis and bike riding, competitive squash, share dealing.

Referees

Available upon request.

Hybrid CV

This is an increasingly popular approach that combines the best of both the chronological CV and the functional CV. A hybrid CV retains much of the fixed order of the chronological CV but there is a lot more emphasis on skills and achievements – sometimes in a separate section.

The hybrid approach is the one that we recommend to most people, in so far as it produces an excellent, clear structure but requires the candidate to really think hard about their achievements and what they have to offer. Obviously there is a limit to how long your CV should be. If you decide to use a hybrid style, you may wish to leave out the detailed responsibilities section and just emphasise the skills, knowledge and abilities.

Bob Brown

Address:	10 Elm Ave London, SW2 4UL
Contact details:	(H) 020 8311 3111 (W) 020 8222 2222

Skills, knowledge, attributes and abilities

Communication skills

In my role as Regional Manager for Next Day Freight I am required to liaise across a broad cross-section of employees. In order to keep employees abreast of company direction and anticipated changes, I implemented briefing sessions held across all shifts once a month. Here I was able to communicate directly with the staff myself and field any questions. Employee satisfaction regarding communication improved from 2.5 to 4.3 over a 12-month period.

Business management

I have a sound knowledge of business management principles. Having completed studies in Management at the University of London, I have continued to keep myself up to date with recent trends and developments by subscribing to journals and magazines. I have also attended several training courses, including the London Business School Executive Development Programme and specialist management courses. Over the past three years, I have implemented ideas gained from my knowledge to restructure our sales force, and supervise the implementation of a new Management Information System and quality improvement programme.

Selling skills

As National Distribution Network Manager for National Petroleum Ltd, I was responsible for developing a merchandising-based franchise package which aimed at converting successful franchisees with other companies to National Petroleum. I developed a programme that targeted the top 100 successful franchisees and, by interviewing a cross-section, identified reasons most would convert. I then developed a selling kit for representatives to use and conducted selling-skills training courses for representatives to develop better levels of skill. I dealt with the top three clients personally and all three converted. Of the remaining 97 franchisees, 70 per cent converted.

Negotiation skills

In my capacity as Regional Manager for Next Day Freight I have been required to address numerous issues regarding workforce planning. This has included outsourcing £2.5 million worth of casual labour, implementing a staff incentive programme and developing a new enterprise agreement. These represented major changes for our existing and often volatile workforce. By developing a committee (which I chaired) involving employee, management and union representatives, we have been able to successfully introduce the required changes without any lost time. Employee satisfaction with working conditions has risen from 1.8 to 4.0 over the past two years.

Tenacity

On my appointment to the position of Regional Manager Next Day Freight I quickly identified potential cost savings in merging our business unit with our sister company's (Parcel Pick Up) business unit worth £10 million. The project to merge the two units was finally realised last month after planning and negotiations spanning more than three years. Anticipated cost savings as a result of the merger are likely to be in the vicinity of £5 billion.

Employment history

Jones Bros Ltd   3/10 to present

Jones Bros is a large national company which owns a range of goods transportation systems. Next Day Freight provides distribution systems for a broad customer base including a range of major UK companies.

Regional Manager for Next Day Freight

Reporting to the General Manager, my major achievements in this position include:

- creation and implementation of a regional business plan addressing major shortfalls in the business
- a successful merger with a £10 million business unit
- restructuring of the entire sales force
- negotiation and implementation of a new enterprise agreement
- complete management restructure
- introduction of new Management Information Systems
- negotiating the outsourcing of £2.5 million p.a. of casual labour
- coordinating the building of a major new depot facility
- implementation of a quantifiable quality improvement programme
- development of a new marketing strategy
- development of a major strategic industrial relations plan to create greater incentive for the workforce
- leading the business unit to its best profit performance.

National Petroleum Ltd

National Distribution Network Manager   3/05 to 2/10

Reporting to the National Planning Manager, my major milestones in this role included:

- a comprehensive review of the sector and development of an integrated business plan for the next century
- development of a new network process to contain the best demographic mix of distribution and marketing
- the development and implementation of a merchandising-based franchise package

- implementation of a business planning process for independent distributors
- a strategic business review of a £300 million subsidiary
- management of the wholesale investment budget to achieve corporate objectives
- successful rationalisation and restructuring of the distributor business to improve the return on investment.

Regional Finance Manager   3/03 to 2/05

Reporting to the Regional Manager, my major responsibilities in this role were the financial performance of the dealer and distributor businesses within the area, and entailed the management of profitability, franchisee selection and administration.

Senior Reseller Area Manager   1/01 to 2/03

Reporting to the Wholesale Network Development Manager.
I was responsible for bottom-line profit, achievement of volume targets, financial management and credit control, tendering for new business and network development.

Marketing, Planning and Economics Officer   2/99 to 12/00

Responsible for SWOT analyses, forecasting and preparation of cost submissions.

Transport Distribution Manager   2/98 to 1/99

Consulting with wholesale fuel distributors.

Rundle and Smith Chartered Accountants   1/96 to 1/98

Team audit work for a range of companies. Reason for leaving: to pursue marketing career.

Qualifications

1993–1995   BA in Management, University of London
Majoring in Accounting and Commercial Law

Professional development

I have attended training courses in the following:

- consultative selling

- analytical skills
- negotiation
- time management
- business management
- executive development programme.

Interests

Swimming, tennis and bike riding, competitive squash, share dealing.

Referees

Available upon request.

Which CV is for me?

Our extensive work has found that recruiters prefer CVs that look conventional. This has been found in studies throughout the world. Most recruiters are conventional people, and they have a clear idea of what they expect to see when they read a CV.

Reading a CV is a bit like walking into a restaurant – we know what to expect. In a restaurant, we know that there will be tables and a menu, that we will be asked for our order and we will have to pay for the food. We might even expect to leave a tip! Receiving an unusual CV would be like walking into the restaurant and seeing no tables or serving staff. We might work out that there is a food vending machine to use, or alternatively we might just walk out. Similarly, we might persevere with an unusual CV, or we might just reject it.

Before we look at some actual examples, we will take a look at what things you should put in your CV.

brilliant tip

Use our 4-S rule – keep it **S**imple, **S**tructured, **S**uccinct and **S**ignificant.

The following is our list of important elements of a CV.

Essential contact details

Always include:

- the name you want to be known by (e.g. James Bright, not James Edward Harold Bright)
- home address
- a telephone number (mobile or landline) at which you can reliably be contacted
- email address.

Only give contact details for places where you are prepared to be contacted by prospective employers. If receiving a call or an email at your current workplace might lead to embarrassing questions from your boss, do not give work contact details.

brilliant tip

You must put your name, address, email address and telephone number on the first page of your CV.

Education and training

If you don't have any formal education obviously you omit these elements and should be thinking of using the functional CV.

Have a look at the ideal candidate you constructed from the job ad in Chapter 4. What qualifications is our potential employer looking for? These qualifications are the ones to focus on.

brilliant tip

Do not bore the reader by listing every qualification you have obtained – keep it to the relevant and impressive stuff.

Go through the list of qualifications you have made and determine which are relevant to the job. List these in order.

Some qualifications, like a university degree, are regarded as relevant information in most circumstances. Other qualifications, such as a first-aid course, may be seen as useful for some jobs, but would look odd being listed for others.

However, if your work experience has superseded your degree, it makes sense to put the work experience before the qualifications. This is what the employer will be most interested in.

Your age will also help you decide what to include and what to leave out. For people in their first five years of work, education is very important and should be listed in reasonable detail. After those first five years be a bit more selective about what you use.

Some qualifications become outdated quickly, so claiming to be a computer expert on the basis of a computing degree obtained 15 years ago will not look very convincing. In this case, evidence of recent work in the field will count for a lot more.

Having said that, a degree shows evidence of critical thinking and intelligence and should not be discarded altogether.

brilliant tip

Be clear, concise and always refer back to the job ad to ensure you're remaining relevant.

The order in which you list qualifications is normally:

- highest postgraduate qualification – Masters or PhD, the subject, and the university at which the degree was taken
- highest undergraduate qualification – the degree, the subject, and the university at which the degree was taken
- secondary school qualifications.

This point may not apply to many people at all but, should you have a PhD, bear in mind that the title of PhDs can often appear to be so obscure or trivially narrow as to detract from a great achievement. Believe us, we have heard the sniggers that sometimes accompany PhD award presentation ceremonies! If you have a very specialised title that is not going to be directly relevant to the job applied for, then stick to the subject discipline name (such as chemistry, physics, English, or psychology).

As you most likely have a degree, it is probably not too important to go into detail about your secondary school results unless they are exceptional. If you have a degree, most employers will credit you with a certain amount of intelligence. What might be useful is to list a few subjects you covered at secondary school, to give an indication of your versatility. For instance, if you have an arts degree, it is probably worth listing 'mathematics, chemistry, statistics' or other numerate subjects studied at secondary school, as this gives an indication of rounded abilities. The opposite applies for science graduates, who might list English and history if applicable.

List any extra languages that you speak, but see our later section on bias.

If there are any particular modules or any special thesis topic, project or other aspect of your studies that are particularly relevant to the job, then mention them here.

With all qualifications, do not assume that the reader will understand what they are. For instance, what do the following mean?

- HSC
- SNVQ
- GCSE
- O-level
- A-level
- cum laude
- Honours
- ACA, RIBA
- Baccalaureate
- City and Guilds
- Grade point average or GPA.

Chances are, some of the above will be a mystery to you. If you are applying for a job in the same country in which you were trained and the qualification system has not changed in the last 10 years, it is safe to assume the employer will understand the meaning of your qualifications. Otherwise, do not assume anyone else will understand your qualifications – if in doubt explain what they mean.

If you gained your qualifications overseas, say what the local equivalent qualification is and, even better, get your qualifications assessed by the relevant government department. If in doubt, contact the local immigration department for assistance.

Look at the following grading systems.

You cannot be sure that 75 per cent from one course is equal to a 'B' in another. A good example comes from UK and Australian universities. In the UK, a 'First' or 'A' is often awarded for scores above 75 per cent, whereas that score in Australia is often a 'two-one' or 'B'. The educational standard is probably not too different, it is just the way people use the scales.

You can be sure that if an employer has any doubts they will tend to think the worst.

brilliant tip

When applying for a job in another state or country, don't assume employers will understand what your qualifications mean. Explain your grades in the employer's local system.

Your work history

Go back to the lists that you have made and try to pick out what in your work history either matches the ideal candidate you have constructed, or looks impressive in its own right.

Unless you are using a functional layout, your work history is the most 'wordy' part of the CV. This is where you have the most scope to influence the reader through your writing style, the words you use, and the way you describe yourself.

Generally list your most recent job first, and then move onto the previous one and so on. If you have a long work history with many different jobs, then we would recommend you restrict listing full details of the positions held in the past 10 years. If there are some earlier jobs that are particularly relevant to the application then these should be included.

One possible exception to the reverse chronological rule might be when your most recent experience is much less relevant to the job you are applying for than earlier roles. This may have happened if you have worked in a non-career role while having a family or following redundancy. You may have switched industry or had a go at starting your own business but decided to return to a previous career. In this case, you could try dividing your work experience into two sections, 'Relevant experience' and 'Other experience'. Obviously, the 'Relevant' section will come before and contain more details than the 'Other' section. You break the rule of chronological order, but you do it in order to prioritise useful information for the recruiter.

For each job you should list:

- dates (in years) of employment
- job title
- employer's name and city location if appropriate
- your responsibilities (keep it brief)
- your achievements in the job.

brilliant tip

Tailor the CV to suit the requirements of the ad and include achievements (not just duties), because this is what will sell you.

The last point on this list is possibly one of the most important. Just providing a job description is not enough. If many applicants have similar backgrounds then the recruiter will be bored to tears and may not even read your CV. What makes you different, more employable, are all of your achievements.

In a study we conducted, recruiters were shown two CVs that were identical except that one described only duties in the job history and the other described achievements. The CV that included achievements was rated much more highly by the recruiters. They were far more impressed with the candidate.

Always emphasise your achievements in each job. A typical job history follows.

Employment history

Trinity Mutual Ltd

Executive Director, Trinity Mutual Master Trust – 3/2010 to present

Key responsibilities include all aspects of the Master Trust, with 25 staff across 4 departments including marketing, client administration, systems and accounting.

President Mutual – 1996 to 2010

Marketing Manager – 2008 to 2009

Key responsibilities included product development and maintenance, marketing and communication of the entire product range of the division.

Assistant General Manager, Financial Products – 2007 to 2008

As above.

Senior Investment Manager, Operations – 2003 to 2007

Key responsibilities included the day-to-day operations of President Funds Management and 'unusual' investments such as leveraged leases, junk bonds, etc.

Fund Manager, Life Fund and Insurance Bonds – 2002 to 2003

Key responsibilities included managing the £3.5 billion Life Fund and the £1.5 billion Insurance Bond Fund, including asset allocation, general management and 'unusual' investments.

Fund Manager, Insurance Bonds – 1999 to 2002

Key responsibilities included managing the new Insurance Bond Fund, including asset allocation, general management and 'unusual' investments.

Actuarial and investment roles – 1996 to 1999

In this period I was engaged in a number of actuarial roles and investment positions within President Mutual.

The achievement focus

Here is the same job history, but this time there is an emphasis on achievements.

Employment history

Trinity Mutual Ltd – 3/2010 to present

Trinity Mutual is a major insurance agency which operates Europe-wide.

Executive Director, Trinity Mutual Master Trust – 3/2010 to present

Key responsibilities include all aspects of the Master Trust, with 25 staff across 4 departments including marketing, client administration, systems and accounting. Major achievements included successful relocation of the administration, accounting and systems areas from external suppliers to head office.

President Mutual Ltd – 1996 to 2010

President Mutual is a major insurance agency which operates UK-wide.

Marketing Manager – 2008 to 2009

Key responsibilities included product development and maintenance, marketing and communication of the entire product range of the division. During this time sales rose by 14 per cent, compared with a 5 per cent rise average in the area.

Assistant General Manager, Financial Products – 2007 to 2008

As above.

Senior Investment Manager, Operations – 2003 to 2007

Key responsibilities included the day-to-day operations of President Funds Management and 'unusual' investments such as leveraged leases, junk bonds, etc.

Fund Manager, Life Fund and Insurance Bonds – 2002 to 2003

Key responsibilities included managing the £3.5 billion Life Fund and the £1.5 billion Insurance Bond Fund, including asset allocation, general management and 'unusual' investments. The fund outperformed all the indexes.

Fund Manager, Insurance Bonds – 1999 to 2002

Key responsibilities included managing the new Insurance Bond Fund, including asset allocation, general management and 'unusual' investments. Major achievements included growing the Fund from £5 million to more than £1 billion.

Actuarial and investment roles – 1996 to 1999

In this period, I was engaged in a number of actuarial roles and investment positions within President Mutual.

Turning responsibilities into achievements

What has this person achieved?

General Manager, Merchandise and Marketing

The major responsibilities in this role included:

- overall accountability for the product, merchandising and promotions for the 100 stores Europe-wide
- product sourcing
- financial control of the sales budget
- managing the team of 12 buying and merchandising staff
- ongoing liaison with state management
- control and accountability of the advertising and marketing needs of the stores.

Major achievements included:

- restructure of the buying department, resulting in increased productivity and lower costs
- changes to the supply chain, resulting in a 4 per cent increase in margins
- development of reporting systems, resulting in enhanced financial planning
- introduction of new offshore merchandise resources
- development and implementation of marketing strategies

- involvement in new stores and refurbishments
- establishment of quality management functions.

You can see that adding the major achievements gives a much more favourable impression of the applicant.

So what constitutes an achievement? Here is our list of criteria for job-related achievements:

- completing something successfully
- an outcome that can be attributed at least in part to you
- something that is measurable (profits, turnover, savings, words per minute)
- something that you can prove to have happened or that can be verified
- making a change or a difference.

Examples of achievements are:

- winning a customer-service award
- improving profits
- introducing a profitable product
- increasing the number of cars serviced per week
- reducing the number of customer complaints
- reducing the turnaround time for orders
- increasing the reliability of a service.

Wherever possible, quantify your achievements. If you managed a team, how big was the team? If you controlled a budget, how much money? If you increased efficiency, by what percentage? It's not always possible to add numbers to achievements, but, where you can, it gives the recruiter a sense of how impressive it was.

You have now rewritten your CV using more positive language, emphasising all your achievements, so it is time to see whether what you have passed the CV fitness test.

Remember from Chapter 2 how employers think about fit in terms of knowledge, skills, abilities and attitudes? Have you worked out:

- what experience is required for the job?
- the skills needed to do the job?
- the abilities that will be required?
- the sort of person/attitudes the employer expects?

Regarding you, have you included in your CV:

- relevant knowledge?
- relevant skills?
- demonstrated compatible abilities?
- demonstrated compatible attitudes?

If the CV passes the fitness test, you should now apply our Gestalt test. The next set of rules is not ours but comes from respected Gestalt psychology. These well-established rules were used to describe visual perception, but they apply equally well to CVs.

The Gestalt rules of CVs

1 **Similarity**: people will group together, as roughly the same, similar jobs and experiences.

2 **Grouping**: people will assume that things that are close together belong together. In other words, if, say, you were in a team that had a success, it puts you close to a success and the success will be associated with you.

3 **Closure**: people look for closure on projects and activities – can you demonstrate that you finished projects you started?

4 **Continuity**: people will assume that things that follow on closely in a similar pattern are part of a longer-term logical development.

Similarity

This can be used effectively on your CV. By emphasising the similarity of your previous jobs to the one you are applying for, you increase the fit between you and the job. Equally, similarity may govern what jobs to include and what to leave out of a CV.

Here is an example of the similarity effect:

Employment history

1995–96	Receptionist, Blue Blot Ink Co.
1996–98	Secretary, Blue Blot Ink Co.
1998–00	Sales Assistant, Jeans R Us
2003–05	Secretary, Hercules Music Company
2005–11	Call Centre Operator, Big Brick Phone Co.
2011–12	Personal Assistant to CEO, Big Brick Phone Co.
2012–present	Personal Assistant to CEO, Slender Phones Ltd

What skills would you describe this person as having? Most people would get the impression from this history that the candidate was a secretary. This is because the terms 'receptionist', 'secretary' and 'personal assistant' all conjure up ideas of similar jobs, whereas 'sales assistant' and 'call centre operator' seem dissimilar. The power of this effect can be seen when you add up the number of years doing the various jobs. This person spent more time (13 years out of 18) not being a secretary.

Grouping

This is a powerful effect. If you were 'close' to some outcome, you will be associated with it. It is a bit like being at the scene of the crime – you automatically become one of the witnesses (and sometimes a suspect). Consider the following two work histories.

Negative grouping

I started in the commodities team, and moved on to sales when the team was disbanded. The sales were outsourced in 2000, when I joined the merchant division.

Positive grouping

I was part of the commodities team that broke all the market records, and then moved to sales, where the group achieved a 25 per cent improvement. This led to my current position in the merchant division.

You can see the power of grouping well here. The first example gives the impression of a loser and the second of a winner, despite the lack of evidence to suggest the candidate was responsible either for any of the successes or the failures.

Research suggests that content is dependent to some extent on the recruiter's perception and this varies according to gender. For example, female recruiters thought men had more work experience while male recruiters perceived that women applicants listed more extracurricular interests. If you provide more space in your résumé to reflect a job, a set of interests or work experience then it's very likely it will be used to define you. Do you really want to be best known for the rest of your life as the top baton twirler at your school? Or the best dog trainer in your village? Or the fastest runner in the local fête's three-legged race? Make sure that every entry counts and reflects what you want to be recognised for.

Closure

Closure is something that many employers will be looking for. They want to see that you can see things through, that you don't quit when the going gets tough. Can you give examples where you completed a project successfully at work? Closure can also be demonstrated by showing that you moved to the next job because your work was completed in the old job, or that you had gained all the personal development likely: 'I moved on because I needed a new challenge having mastered my old job.'

Continuity

This relates most obviously to gaps in career history. We will spend some more time considering this later. However, it is worth pointing out here that most employers want to see continuity in employment. Continuity has two aspects. First, have you been continuously employed over the years and, secondly, does your work history combine to tell a logical story or does it appear random? The following examples illustrate this point:

Continuous employment, but discontinuous types of job

1995–96	Receptionist, Blue Blot Ink Co.
1996–98	Assistant Chemist, Blue Blot Ink Co.
1998–00	Sales Assistant, Jeans R Us
2003–05	Product Packer, Hercules Music Company
2005–11	Stores Administrator, Big Brick Phone Co.
2011–12	Sales Representative, Big Brick Phone Co.
2012–present	Glazier, Heritage Doors Ltd

Continuous employment, and reasonably continuous types of job

1995–96	Receptionist, Blue Blot Ink Co.
1996–98	Secretary, Blue Blot Ink Co.
1998–00	Sales Assistant, Jeans R Us
2003–05	Secretary, Hercules Music Company
2005–11	Call Centre Operator, Big Brick Phone Co.
2011–12	Personal Assistant to CEO, Big Brick Phone Co.
2012–present	Personal Assistant to CEO, Slender Phones Ltd

From these examples, it can be seen clearly that the story of the first candidate's working life is a very confused and mixed one. It doesn't create a great impression. The second candidate's history tells a story of steady advancement (and therefore achievement) in the secretarial area. It is a much more positive story.

Now you know all about the Gestalt laws, use them to guide what goes into your CV and what does not, how to word your job history and how to present your CV. Once your CV passes the fitness test and the Gestalt test, you are ready to put the icing on the cake! In the next chapter, we discuss some techniques that we have demonstrated in our research to be effective.

CHAPTER 9

Presenting your CV

We have already touched on some basic points about the best way to present your CV – we've seen that recruiters prefer simple typefaces and plain white paper. In this chapter, we look at successful presentation in more detail.

Layout

The first thing to say about the layout of your CV is do not put the words 'Résumé' or 'Curriculum Vitae' on the top of your CV. Quite apart from insulting the reader – what else could the document be? – it is a waste of valuable space.

At the top of the first page of your CV, put your full name (or the name you wish to be known by). It should be in bold type and at a size that is clearly bigger than the rest of the type on the page so it stands out – perhaps 16pt or slightly larger. It may also be centred on the page to increase the impact. Leave several lines of white space below this heading, before you list your personal contact details.

Aligned on the left side of your page, give your address. Use the right-hand side on the same lines to give your telephone and fax numbers. There are no hard and fast rules (i.e. evidence) to support the layout of this information and the alternative is to centre all of this information. We suggest you try each format and decide which you prefer.

The remainder of your CV appears in the following order:

- education details should come next (though there are variations on this)
- professional associations
- work history
- references (if you include them) come last, according to convention.

Headings

Headings have to be consistent in appearance. They must all be the same font and size. In the example given on page 120, there are three different levels of headings. The applicant's name is given in Arial, 20 points in size, and is in bold. The major sections 'Education' and 'Work history' are 14 points in size, in bold. Subheadings under 'Work history' are in 12 point italics, and the text is 10 point. Making the same type of headings look the same is another example of the Gestalt law of similarity. The reader finds it easy to see the separate sections.

White space and grouping

Aim to leave plenty of white space on your CV. If you put too much writing on a page, your CV will be hard to read and look cluttered. You should also allow a generous margin of about 2 centimetres or more on all sides.

▶ brilliant example

White space can be used to indicate that things close to each other belong together. In the example, there is plenty of space between the person's contact details and their education. There are smaller gaps between their school and university, and then there is a larger gap again between education and work history. The size of the gaps tells the reader that the things close together are all related. The larger gap indicates to the reader they are moving on to some different type of information.

Font

Use the same font throughout. Here are some good and bad examples:

The fast cat jumped over the lazy dog. (Arial)

The fast cat jumped over the lazy dog. (Times New Roman)

The fast cat jumped over the lazy dog. (Tahoma)

The fast cat jumped over the lazy dog. (Bookman)

The fast cat jumped over the lazy dog. (Baskerville Bold)

The fast cat jumped over the lazy dog. (Brush Script)

THE FAST CAT JUMPED OVER THE LAZY DOG. (STENCIL)

The first two are both acceptable fonts; the second two are less acceptable, but still okay; the last three are definitely not suitable. Fashions in fonts change as quickly as, well, fashion! However, there are some important considerations. First, choose what is called a universal font – these are ones that are installed on all computer systems regardless of manufacturer (e.g. Apple Macs and PCs); they are: Arial, Georgia, Lucida Console, Palatino, Tahoma, Times New Roman, Trebuchet, Verdana. Using a font that may not be present on the recruiter's computer risks the document formatting being messed up, and so should be avoided. These fonts are also 'conventional' looking and easy to read. Verdana is likely to be the best bet (and it looks like this). We will tell you why.

Research has shown that Times and Arial are read faster than Courier, Schoolbook and Georgia. Fonts at the 12 point size were read faster than fonts at the 10 point size. In general, however, Arial, Courier and Georgia are perceived as the most legible. For font attractiveness, Georgia is perceived as being more attractive than Arial, Courier and Comic, while Times is perceived as more attractive than Courier. Overall, Verdana is the most preferred font, while Times was the least preferred. Thus it seems that the Georgia and Times serif fonts are considered more attractive, but they are generally less preferred. Of the fonts studied, Verdana appears to be the best overall font choice. Besides being the most preferred, it is read fairly quickly and is perceived as being legible.

Bullet points or continuous prose?

We did some research to see whether recruiters had a preference for work histories presented as bullet points or as continuous prose (that is, as a series of normal sentences). The results were not straightforward. Recruiters tended to prefer candidates to write complete sentences, but if the CV had been rewritten by a recruitment agency, they tended to prefer bullet points!

So what should you do?

Bullet points are quick and easy to read, and look attractive on the page, as long as there are not too many of them. The risk with bullet points is that people tend to be too brief and the bullet point becomes meaningless. For example:

I have good working knowledge of Word and Excel and some experience of PowerPoint.

Compare this with:

● Word, Excel, PowerPoint.

The first sentence provides more information than the bullet point.

brilliant tip

If you are going to use bullet points, make sure that they are meaningful.

Finally, it is worth noting that writing complete sentences allows you to show off your communication skills if your spelling and grammar are good.

Other important layout and presentation issues

Here are some other points to keep in mind:

- You should not use underlined headings as it tends to look messy, and headings may also be misread by computer scanners. (More about this in Part 4.)

- Do not use both sides of the paper. People may forget to photocopy or scan both sides.

- You must have your CV laser-printed. Using old or cheaper printers is not acceptable now that high-quality laser printers are commonly available.

- Do not use colour in your CV. It often looks tacky and cannot be photocopied easily.

- Do not put clip-art, cartoons or other illustrations on your CV. (Remember our advice about wacky CVs?)

- Use high-quality paper that is white (other colours may not scan or copy well).

- If you are sending out photocopies, ensure that the quality of the copy is excellent (a good copy is almost indistinguishable from an original).

- Do not fold your CV – buy an A4 envelope.

- When sending your CV electronically, unless otherwise instructed save it as a PDF document. This will preserve the formatting. Word processors have a nasty habit of changing the formatting slightly from version to version and from computer to computer.

Over the page is an example of a well set-out CV, followed by the same CV set out poorly.

CV example 1

IAN GREGORY CHAPPELL

360 Edgecliff Avenue
Wakefield
West Yorkshire
WF4 2NO

Telephone: 01924 523124 (home)
01924 523421 (work)
07803 644644 (mobile)
Fax: 01924 523422 (work)
Email: igchappell@hotmail.com

Education

1997 – 2002   St Mark of the Blessed Taylor High School, Leeds
2003 – 2007   Electrical Engineering, Salford University
                  First Class Honours

Work history

2012 – Present   **Telstra**   **Wakefield**

Operations Manager

I am currently responsible for ...

2007 – 2012   **Optus**   **Leeds**

An international telecommunications company.

Communications Engineer

I was responsible ...

Senior Communications Manager

I did ...

CV example 2

CONFIDENTIAL CV OF:

Name: Ian Gregory Chappell
Address: 360 Edgecliff Avenue, Wakefield, West Yorkshire, WF4 2NO
Telephone: 01924 523124
01924 523421 (work)
07803 644644 (mobile)
Fax: 01924 523422 (work)
email: igchappell@hotmail.com

Education

1997 – 2002

St Mark of the Blessed Taylor High School, Leeds

2003 – 2007

Electrical Engineering, Salford University, First Class Honours

Work history

2007 – 2012	Optus	Leeds

An international telecommunications company

Communications Engineer

I was responsible ...

Senior Communications Manager

I did ...

2012 – Present	Telstra	Wakefield

Operations Manager

I am currently responsible for ...

Using white space

Which of the following CV layouts looks the best?

CV 1

CV 2

CV 3

Anthony Hancock
2 Railway Cuttings, East Cheam, Surrey, CR7 2OT — Telephone (020) 8234 5678 — Email address: tony@bdoner.co.uk

Career objective
I am looking for a busy, entry-level position in administration that utilises my computing and organisational skills while enabling me to learn about a business from the ground up.

Skills, experience and personal attributes
Communication skills
- I have been developing my public speaking skills while competing in the Rostrum public speaking competitions. This experience has given me the confidence to express myself clearly and confidently.
- As a finalist in the Rostrum public speaking competition I was invited to present to no fewer than 200 people. I regularly use my written communication skills in the composing of correspondence and promotional material for the Interact Club.

Customer relations skills
- While at Harvey Norman, I have helped many customers, resulting in my being awarded 'Employee of the Month' five times. I take time to listen to customers, identify their needs and then recommend products that are most suitable.
- While at Harvey Norman I have attended a two-day training course on Customer Service Skills.

Time management skills
- While completing my A Levels I have held down a part-time position at Harvey Norman as well as being Secretary to the Interact Club. These extra-curricular activities have put additional demands on my time, and without careful planning my school work would have suffered.
- I have never missed a school deadline or needed an extension to complete work. To make the best use of my time I schedule it and complete tasks in order of priority. I believe these time management skills will transfer well to the workplace.

Computer skills
- During my last year at secondary school I have completed a course in Computer Studies. This has included use of the following packages: Excel, Word for Windows, Access and PowerPoint. I was ranked second in my class for Computer Studies and feel that I am highly proficient in use of the packages.
- As a keen computer user at home I am also familiar with Netscape and Eudora.

Education
2010 A Levels, Tottenham High School
Subjects: English, Mathematics, Economics, Geography
2010 Computer Studies
2009 – 2010 Customer Service Skills, In-House Harvey Norman
Academic achievements
Nov 2010 Ranked top student in Economics at Tottenham High School
Nov 2010 Rostrum Public Speaking Competition Finalist

Employment history
Feb 2009 – Dec 2010 Secretary, Interact Club, Tottenham High School
- taking minutes of weekly meetings, composing and typing outgoing correspondence
- organising mail-outs to students on club activities, actioning in-coming correspondence
- typing up minutes from Interact meetings
- awarded with school prize for community involvement
- membership increased from 10 to 17 members following mailings that I initiated
- all in-coming mail dealt with within seven days of receipt

Feb 2009 – Dec 2010 Service Assistant (part-time), Harvey Norman, Oxford Street
- helping customers with location of products, explaining different features of products to customers
- dealing with customer complaints when products returned
- serving customers at cash registers and stocking shelves with products
- 'Employee of the Month' May 2009, Nov 2009, Feb 2010, July 2010, Sep 2010 (based on customer nomination)
- awarded employee with 'Best knowledge – bathroom fittings' by Caroma (supplier)

Interests and activities
Meeting new people, computing, public speaking, regular blood donor
Feb 2009 – Dec 2010 Interact Club

Referees
Mr Sidney James
Manager, Harvey Norman
(020) 8222 3333

Mr Kenneth Williams
Head Teacher, Tottenham High School
(020) 8919 1667

CV 4

CV 5

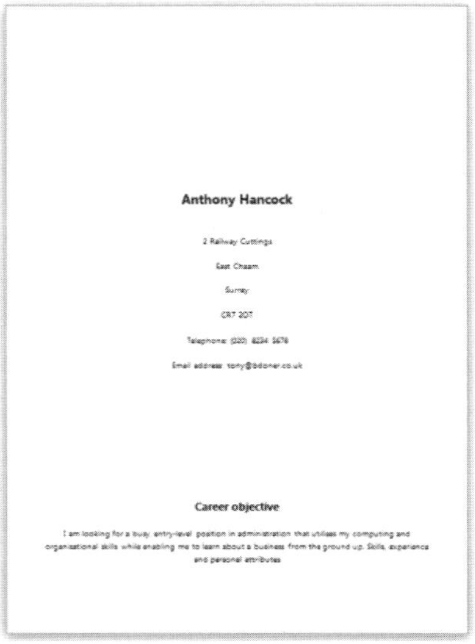

Anthony Hancock

2 Railway Cuttings

East Cheam

Surrey

CR7 2OT

Telephone: (020) 8234 5678

Email address: tony@bdoner.co.uk

Career objective

I am looking for a busy, entry-level position in administration that utilises my computing and organisational skills while enabling me to learn about a business from the ground up. Skills, experience and personal attributes

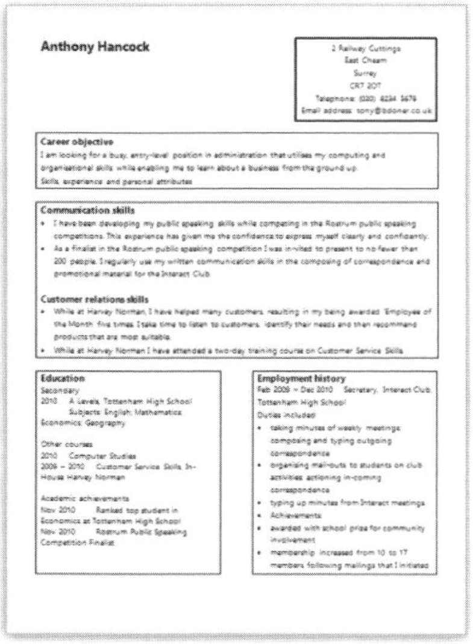

Anthony Hancock

2 Railway Cuttings
East Cheam
Surrey
CR7 2OT
Telephone: (020) 8234 5678
Email address: tony@bdoner.co.uk

Career objective
I am looking for a busy, entry-level position in administration that utilises my computing and organisational skills while enabling me to learn about a business from the ground up.
Skills, experience and personal attributes

Communication skills
- I have been developing my public speaking skills while competing in the Rostrum public speaking competitions. This experience has given me the confidence to express myself clearly and confidently.
- As a finalist in the Rostrum public speaking competition I was invited to present to no fewer than 200 people. I regularly use my written communication skills in the composing of correspondence and promotional material for the Interact Club.

Customer relations skills
- While at Harvey Norman, I have helped many customers, resulting in my being awarded 'Employee of the Month' five times. I take time to listen to customers, identify their needs and then recommend products that are most suitable.
- While at Harvey Norman I have attended a two-day training course on Customer Service Skills.

Education
Secondary
2010 A Levels, Tottenham High School
Subjects: English; Mathematics
Economics; Geography

Other courses
2010 Computer Studies
2009 – 2010 Customer Service Skills, In-House Harvey Norman

Academic achievements
Nov 2010 Ranked top student in Economics at Tottenham High School
Nov 2010 Rostrum Public Speaking Competition Finalist

Employment history
Feb 2009 – Dec 2010 Secretary, Interact Club, Tottenham High School
Duties included:
- taking minutes of weekly meetings; composing and typing outgoing correspondence
- organising mail-outs to students on club activities; actioning in-coming correspondence
- typing up minutes from Interact meetings
- Achievements
- awarded with school prize for community involvement
- membership increased from 10 to 17 members following mailings that I initiated

CV 6

We think the outstanding winner is CV 2. The layout achieves a nice balance between the amount of information provided and the overall neat and tidy easy-to-read appearance. Secondly, this CV has used the idea that things that are close together will be assumed to belong together. In CV 2, you can see clearly the different sections. This makes the CV look more logical and structured – and we cannot even read what it is saying! Notice how this CV leaves larger margins at the top and bottom and on the left and right.

CV 3 is not too bad, although the structure is a little less clear. Ideally the CV should have definite sections – name, contact details, training/ education, job history/skills. On this CV, it looks as though the name and contact details are all bunched together.

CV 1 is not too bad, but notice how the eye is drawn to the empty white space at the top right. It looks as though a photograph or picture has been removed. This layout might be a good idea if you are submitting an electronic CV or if you think that the CV is likely to be scanned into a computer. The alignment of the text on the left, and the fact that each new section starts at the left-hand margin, makes it less likely that a computer will misread your CV.

CV 5 is an example of people taking the idea of 'white space' a bit too far. Here the CV looks to contain very little information, and it suggests either that the candidate has little to offer, or that we are in for about 10 pages of artistic minimalism!

CVs 4 and 6 are shocking! CV 4 is an example of what happens when the writer has not thought through what they want to say and therefore attempts to cram in as much as possible. Remember, less can often be more with CVs. The look of this CV is off-putting and suggests to the reader that they might need a couple of stiff drinks to help them get all the way through it. This layout can be justified only when the CV is being used for a proposal where a very strict page limit on the overall application is demanded, or perhaps where a candidate has been specifically asked (perhaps after interview) to provide a much more detailed background document. For the rest of you, if your CV resembles CV 4, rewrite it immediately!

CV 6 is a mess. The boxes around the text are distracting and, although they clearly indicate the various sections, the same effect can be achieved in a less heavy-handed manner with judicious use of white space (as in CV 2). Furthermore, these boxes may stuff up a computer scan of the CV. Resist the temptation to show off your skills with the Draw or Insert Picture commands on your word processor.

PART 2

The icing on the cake

So now you have a CV, beautifully set out and crammed with achievements. You've baked your cake! Next, we show you how to improve your CV even further, by putting the icing on the cake. In this section, we explore the techniques that have been shown by our research to be successful in impressing recruiters.

CHAPTER 10

Mind your language!

We have spent a lot of time discussing just how important it is to emphasise your results and successes on your CV, but this should not be at the expense of making sure the language on your CV is absolutely spot on.

Word power

When you list your achievements, pay attention to how you write them because the words you choose can have a huge influence on recruiters. Recruiters will judge your CV on how well you communicate, so choosing the right words is very important.

Think back to the beginning when we were discussing the importance of selling yourself. The words listed below are examples of good 'selling' words.

overcame	achieved	enlarged	developed	discovered
controlled	managed	delivered	reorganised	won
applied	defeated	eliminated	engineered	overhauled
presented	founded	instigated	created	directed
attracted	led	initiated	established	enjoyed
contributed	modified	specialised	expanded	repaired
improved	analysed	co-ordinated	trained	organised
guided	conducted	implemented	built	designed
persuaded	helped	proved	utilised	simplified

investigated	completed	compiled	demonstrated	accomplished
transformed	introduced	finalised	headed	constructed
supervised	illustrated	outlined	selected	monitored

Words that can boost the power even more include:

quickly	successfully	rapidly	carefully	decisively
competently	resourcefully	capably	efficiently	consistently
effectively	positively	co-operatively	selectively	creatively
assertively	energetically	enthusiastically	responsibly	flexibly

Words with negative connotations should be avoided if possible. They include:

avoided	failed	succumbed	relied	conflicted
tried	disciplined	attempted	abandoned	unsuccessfully
lost	dismissed	withdrew	relinquished	argued

brilliant tip

Write positively. It's all about Attitude!

Clichés

There are some warnings here and the first is beware of clichés. Clichés are overworn phrases that become meaningless and irritating. For instance, 'Have a nice day', or 'In a packed programme tonight …', or 'Our world exclusive', or 'Unaccustomed as I am to public speaking …'. Unfortunately, the world of work has a peculiar love of clichés, so it is difficult to know when you are 'over-egging the pudding' (to use a cliché).

brilliant tip

Avoid putting clichés in your CV. At best they will be disregarded, at worst they will irritate.

Below are a few examples that are still okay to use.

▶ **brilliant** example

Total quality	Beware not to overuse this term (e.g. 'total added value', or 'total global communication', etc.) or the word 'quality'
Added value	(Yuk! But some people appear to like it)
Global space	As in 'HR space' or the 'outer space'
Downsizing	
Rightsizing	
Outsourcing	
Focus	As in 'customer focus' or 'team focus' (but not 'total focus')

Now, read through your list of achievements and look closely at each word you have used. Is there another word that might make you look more impressive? If so, replace the word with the more positive one.

Technical language

Many jobs in the legal, medical, scientific and computing areas have lots of jargon words associated with them. It is always very difficult to know when and where to use such words. You can be sure it is safe to use words or phrases that appear in the job advertisement or description. If the employer uses simplified words or phrases to describe some technical aspect of a job, then you should also stick to the simplified words. However, in this case it is permissible to provide more technical examples to illustrate your point.

For instance, if the advertisement says 'high-level statistical knowledge required' it is permissible to include a statement such as 'I have a very high level of statistical knowledge, including the use of multiple regression, analysis of variance and structural equation modelling techniques'. The first part of the sentence uses the same language as the advertisement, and the second part goes into more detail. If you include only the second part of the sentence, it is possible that the person reading the CV initially may not have the technical knowledge to appreciate that 'multiple regression, analysis of variance and structural equation modelling techniques' are high-level statistical techniques, and so your CV may be rejected.

Remember, there is a fundamental imbalance between the applicant and the employer at this stage. It is permissible for the employers to use jargon terms that send you to the library seeking clarification, but do not be tempted to throw your own different jargon back at them – employers do not want to visit the library!

Me, myself and I

There is a heated debate about whether you should include the personal pronoun 'I' on your CV. Our view is this is not a black or white issue but one of style. If every sentence begins with an 'I' it is simply poor style and you will be crowned the king or queen of Iam. Use 'I' judiciously and vary it with shortened sentences that begin with the verb – e.g. instead of 'I planned the Mad Hatter's tea party' use 'Planned the Mad Hatter's party'. If anybody says that use of 'I' is egotistical, ask yourself what a CV is about, if it is not about you and your achievements.

Some useful texts that can assist you more fully in this regard include:

- *The Elements of Style* (Allyn & Bacon)
- *Longman Student Grammar of Spoken and Written English* (Longman)
- *Fowler's Modern English Usage* (Oxford University Press)
- *The Oxford Dictionary for Writers and Editors* (Oxford University Press).

CHAPTER 11

Using competency statements

What is a competency statement?

Put simply, a competency statement briefly outlines the knowledge, skills, attitudes and abilities you possess.

Think back to Chapter 2 where we talked about 'fit'. We showed you how employers think about jobs in terms of the knowledge required to do the job, the skills required to do the job, the attitude that is required, and the abilities required.

A competency statement should address all these points, and should serve to increase the perception of fit between you and the job in the employer's mind.

brilliant tip

Include competency statements and back up with examples.

Below are some example statements created to emphasise some quality that an employer is seeking:

▶ brilliant examples

Highly motivated: I have a proven track record of achievement, both within university and through extra-curricular activities. I have won numerous awards throughout my academic career, but have still managed to maintain a balance with social activities.

Sales market knowledge: I keep in touch with the market by reading sales journals and magazines, as well as visiting supermarkets and other points of sale. Last year, I completed a research project entitled 'What makes a supermarket tick: best placement or best product?', which looked at the dynamics of product placement in stores and the impact on sales.

Organisational skills: As a person who is involved in many different activities, I have developed excellent organisational skills to ensure that I plan my time effectively. This enables me to achieve maximum output in minimum time, as well as handle a number of activities simultaneously.

Energetic: I am a person who is always on the go, as I am involved in a number of activities. These range from academic to work-related to sporting, particularly team sports. I am an outgoing person and enjoy being an active member of numerous clubs and associations.

Communication skills: My diverse range of experiences at university, work and in extra-curricular activities has enabled me to acquire strong verbal and written communication skills. As an outgoing person, I have also had numerous opportunities to develop my interpersonal skills to a high level.

Responsible: As a person who has always been involved in a range of activities, I have developed a responsible and mature approach to any task that I undertake, or situation that I am presented with. I believe that these assets will stand me in good stead for any future positions that I undertake.

You can see from looking at all of the statements that each one addresses one aspect of a job. The words in bold are the words that the candidate has realised are critical components of the job from analysing the job advertisement.

Here is a job advertisement with the keywords in bold:

GRADUATE SALES ANALYST
Transform your career!

Step up to an organisation that's **really on the move globally**, with consumer and pharmaceutical products that consistently set a new standard for excellence at the world-class level.

As a crucial member of our 'Household Products' sales team, you will be working with leading brands. Your exceptional analytical ability will enable you to analyse market data, and **working closely with Account Managers** help build our brands in the marketplace. **Carefully monitoring** sales of our products, and our competitors', will be of prime importance. You will be more than just a 'number cruncher' in this role – you will develop an intimate understanding of how the grocery trade operates: both from the retailer's and manufacturer's perspective.

We're looking for a person who is **motivated, keen to stay in touch with the marketplace**, and who can ably provide tactical support in achieving specific objectives.

Requirements for the position are tertiary qualifications in business, marketing or a related discipline. You may have some sales or retail experience, and a strong desire to pursue a sales career. A track record of achievement is essential!

You can see from an analysis of the advertisement what sorts of qualities they are looking for in the job:

- 'really on the move globally' means energetic
- 'working closely with Account Managers' means communication and organisation skills
- 'carefully monitoring' means responsible
- 'motivated' and 'achievement' mean highly motivated
- 'keen to stay in touch with the marketplace' means sales market knowledge.

The competency statement for each quality is simply a short sentence or two saying why you have those qualities. You can see how these sorts of statements try to emphasise the fit between the candidate and job more directly than a mere job history.

Do they work?

We were not at all convinced that such statements would be effective, but were amazed to find that, when we included them on CVs, they boosted our candidates' chances by as much as 30 per cent. In one study, one candidate's CV that did not include these statements was not short-listed by any of our professional recruiters. When we put competency statements on the CV, one in three recruiters said they would interview the candidate! For another candidate, when the statements were included on the CV every recruiter said they would interview the candidate, whereas only 8 out of 10 said they would interview the candidate when the statements were missing.

We were so surprised by these results, we did another study to check whether we had made a mistake. We got exactly the same results.

brilliant tip

Always include as much quantifiable data as possible when listing achievements.

Where should you put them on a CV?

We have tried placing these statements at the end of the CV, before the 'referees' section, and we have placed them at the beginning after the applicant's name. We've put them on the second page, and we've put them in the covering letter, all with exactly the same results. It does not seem to matter where you put them, as long as they are there. We usually put them under the heading 'Knowledge, skills and abilities'.

Why do they work?

There are probably several reasons why they are so successful. First, you are picking up on the attributes the employer thinks are important and addressing each of them – it's a bit like answering an interview question like 'Tell me, do you have any sales market knowledge?' You are talking the employer's language.

Secondly, you are making it easier for the employer to see the fit between you and the job, because you have taken the trouble to point out all the things in common. It may also make it easier for a computer scanner to pick out any keywords.

Finally, the very fact you've put this extra section on your CV shows you have thought a bit more deeply about the job and how you would fit it well. It makes you stand out from all those candidates who just list their skills and qualifications as if to say 'take it or leave it'.

Are they a bit over the top?

Very probably yes, but it doesn't seem to matter. In fact we found that the more competency statements we included on a CV, the more likely it was that the candidate was shortlisted for interview!

I bet this 'trick' doesn't fool experienced recruiters!

Yes and no. While it is true that younger or inexperienced recruiters are the most likely to be influenced by these statements, we found that even older and very experienced recruiters tended to short-list CVs containing these statements more often than standard CVs.

How do you write a competency statement?

First revisit Chapter 4, which tells you how to analyse a job advertisement. Then follow these easy steps:

1   Pick out the key qualities that the employer is looking for from the job ad. Qualities listed in Chapter 4 such as 'motivated', 'great communicator' and so forth are common.

2   Go back through the templates of you and your achievements that you made earlier. How can you demonstrate these desired qualities? Have a look at the example competency statements in this chapter for some ideas on how to do it.

3   Read through what you've written carefully. Can you justify what you are claiming? If not, omit the statement – it is not acceptable to lie. If you are found out (which is likely), you could be fired from the job you get. Does the statement look really weak or unexceptional? If it does, omit it or strengthen it by giving concrete examples. Examples of statements that are probably too weak include: 'I get on well with people' (strengthen by giving examples), 'I am a likeable person' (strengthen by giving examples).

If you're having trouble coming to grips with this idea, look at the samples at the end of the text. These outline the types of competency statements to use in more detail.

brilliant tip

Include competency statements on your CV!

The more competency statements you put on your CV, the more chance you have of being short-listed.

	Competency 1	Competency 2, etc.
What did you do?		
What was the context?		
How do you know it was successful?		
Does it convince the reader without a shadow of a doubt?		

CHAPTER 12

Telling tales

ere is a new way of writing résumés that we have developed for job hunters based upon story-telling. Stories, or narratives as they are sometimes called, are increasingly being rediscovered as an effective way of communicating with others. Some medical training now includes narrative medicine – listening to patients' stories because it is believed it leads to more accurate diagnoses. In employment interviews, asking candidates to provide examples of when they demonstrated a particular skill in the workplace is really just an invitation to tell a story. So let's take the logical step and include stories on the CV. The stories you develop in this chapter can then be included in your competency statements on your CV. As a bonus, by the end of this chapter you will also have prepared a lot of highly memorable material to use in the interview as well.

A test to start with

Here's a test for you. We want you to read the following paragraph and then we'll ask you some questions about it.

Candidate 1

> I am really good at customer service. I think that customer service is really important. It is important that customers are served well and their needs are met. I have done customer service training and want to continue to keep my skills up in this important area. If customers don't get service they don't come back. In my current role we always put the customer first.

Questions

1 Is this candidate good at customer service?
2 Have they convinced you they would be good at customer service?
3 What evidence did they present in support of their claim?

Candidate 2

I am really good at customer service. This is because I always go the extra mile to understand the customers' needs and then I try my hardest to meet their expectations. For instance, two weeks ago I had a customer come into our store who was complaining that her appliance had slipped. I decided quickly that my task was to understand whether or not the customer had received our on-site training in how to stop the appliance vibrating at the wrong time. It turned out that she was unaware of this training service, but indicated that she was willing to try the training before returning the appliance. So I organised for our trainers to visit her later the very same day. The result was her appliance stopped slipping and she wrote in praise of our helpful and prompt service. This is a good illustration of my commitment to outstanding customer service.

Questions

1 Is this candidate good at customer service?
2 Have they convinced you they would be good at customer service?
3 What evidence did they present in support of their claim?

Which of these candidates presents the stronger case for short-listing?

The answer is that candidate 2 did a much better job, and the reason they did a better job was that they presented their claim clearly and logically. However, even more importantly, they told a story about a time when they demonstrated the key skill. The story about the customer with a slipping appliance is likely to stick in your mind for some time, whereas the empty self-aggrandising statements and opinions of candidate 1 will be forgotten quickly.

Candidate 2 stands out because we naturally learn and remember stories well: it is a fundamental part of our nature. Stories are also good news because we naturally have a facility to recall them over long periods of time, whereas claims, assertions and statements tend to be forgotten. So not only are you more likely to stick in the mind of the recruiter, by telling your own stories, but you are also much more likely to be able to remember them yourself, even under the icy glare of an interview panel. So the lesson is to include as many stories on the CV as possible.

Another bonus of using stories is that they are tailor-made for one of the most popular approaches to interviewing used today – the behavioural interview. In a behavioural interview, the interviewer prompts the candidate to provide examples of a time when … the candidate demonstrated excellent customer service, showed leadership, managed to beat it down with a stick, etc. If you have already prepared a range of stories and included some on your résumé, you are already not only more likely to be short-listed, but also halfway to answering all the interview questions as well.

The elements of a good story

A good story needs a plot, it needs characters and it needs detail.

Consider the following:

> A couple of kids go to school and they get into some trouble with the other students and also with some of the teachers. However, after a while they demonstrate that they are not bad and the good teachers like them.

That is hardly the stuff of best-sellers! What is missing crucially from this story is detail and characters. If we name the school kids as Harry Potter, Ron Weasley and Hermione Granger, and the school as Hogwarts, we become a little more engaged. Then if we describe the teachers and the trouble they get into in more detail, you never know, but you might have a modest best-seller on your hands!

The same goes for stories we tell on CVs and also the ones we will subsequently tell in the interview. The trouble is, most of us tend to talk in generalities and skip the details – so we write or say in the interview things like 'I am great at customer service, for instance I had this customer once who was complaining, and I got them to stop complaining by providing some training'. Essentially this is candidate 2's story, but it is a lot less compelling when stripped of all the little details that make the story credible.

☼ brilliant tip

When choosing your stories to use on your CV (and also for the interview) ensure they pass the following test:

- **What** is the **point** you are trying to make?
- **What** happened?
- **Why** did it happen?
- **Where** did it happen?
- **When** did it happen?
- **Who** was there?
- **What** were their **names**? (If you are worried about maintaining confidentiality, work out some aliases to use, and include the phrase 'For the sake of confidentiality, I will call them "X"'). Using names helps people follow a story, and by acknowledging confidentiality issues, you will get bonus points for your professional approach).

Choose the right plot

It is amazing how often job seekers will refer to stories or launch into them at interview without realising the story does not have a happy ending. You know the sort of thing: 'I demonstrated excellent customer service last week by listening to an irate customer to ensure I understood her.' 'And what happened?' (asks the recruiter). 'Oh, the manager had to call the police to separate us after the brawl broke out into the high street.'

Christopher Booker (author of *The Seven Basic Plots: Why We Tell Stories*) says there are seven essential plots for stories. These are the stories with our very rough summaries of each one:

1 **Rags to riches** – you go from nothing to success

2 **Overcoming the monster** – you face a major challenge and win

3 **The Quest** – you set a goal to achieve and manage it

4 **Voyage and Return** – you discover new things and learn from them

5 **Comedy** – you are deluded about the true realities but eventually see the light

6 **Tragedy** – you make a bad decision that sets you on a path to destruction

7 **Rebirth** – you have a dark period of suffering or stagnation and awake renewed and refreshed.

The point is, you should check your story to make sure it is not a tragedy, or even a comedy. The other ones are all positive stories, or should be if you work on your story enough. Recruiters will generally be impressed if you have worked from nothing to success, have overcome a major challenge, achieved a goal, tried things, learned and improved, or have refocused and come back even stronger. It is crucial to think through your stories very carefully to ensure that they increase the fit between you and the job. A little bit of thought and preparation at this stage will pay dividends on your CV and also in your interview. Effectively what you are doing is creating your own script for the CV and the interview that is not only going to impress the recruiter, but will also reduce your nerves because you know what you want to say.

First and last is the most important

So telling stories seems to help embed you more deeply in the memories of recruiters. There is another insight from cognitive psychology we can draw on to make our stories even more memorable, and to illustrate this, here is another test for you. We want you to look at the following numbers and memorise them:

7 16 191 312 0 50 53 91 87 54 23 0 11 17 0 34 32 22 19 64 86 14 12 8

Now without looking try to recall the numbers.

We would bet that most readers would be able to recall the first few numbers, then things get a little tricky, but they can also remember the last one or two as well. In other words, we remember the first and last things presented to us. We can make use of that in stories by making sure that we make the point we want to make twice – at the beginning and end of our stories.

PREP – the gold standard of communication

If you look back on candidate 2's story it follows exactly this structure. In fact it follows the structure of the sound bite, and the following formula is pure gold when it comes to effective communication. It was taught to Jim by a media communications expert called Paul Griffiths, who used to present *The Money Programme* on BBC2. David Winter (one of our authors) has modified it when using it for students in his careers service. The formula we use is:

- **P**oint
- **R**eason
- **E**vidence
- **P**oint forward

If we take candidate 2's story and break it down using the formula, we get the following:

Point	I am really good at customer service.
Reason	This is because I always go the extra mile to understand the customers' needs and then I try my hardest to meet their expectations.

Evidence	For instance, two weeks ago I had a customer come into our store who was complaining that her appliance had slipped. I decided quickly that my task was to understand whether or not the customer had received our on-site training in how to stop the appliance vibrating at the wrong time. It turned out that she was unaware of this training service, but indicated that she was willing to try the training before returning the appliance. So I organised for our trainers to visit her later the very same day. The result was her appliance stopped slipping and she wrote to us in praise of our helpful and prompt service.
Point forward	I will always take time to find out the background to a customer's complaint because it's much easier to work out what will turn them into a satisfied customer again.

If you listen to politicians you'll find them using this formula all the time. For instance, I bet you have heard this one: 'My government is the best this country has had because we are great economic managers. For instance, inflation, unemployment and interest rates are at historically low levels, proving this government is the best we've ever had.' The classic PREP formula. However, there is an even stronger formula that combines PREP with another well-known formula.

PREP-STAR – the platinum standard of communication

The STAR of PREP-STAR stands for:

- **S**ituation
- **T**ask
- **A**ction
- **R**esult

The full PREP-STAR formula is:

- **P**oint
- **R**eason
- **E**vidence
  - **S**ituation
  - **T**ask
  - **A**ction
  - **R**esult
- **P**oint forward

If we go back and look at candidate 2's story we can see each element of this formula in action.

Point	I am really good at customer service.
Reason	Because I always go the extra mile to understand the customers' needs and then I try my hardest to meet their expectations.
Evidence	
Situation	For instance, two weeks ago I had a customer come into our store who was complaining that her appliance had slipped.
Task	I decided quickly that my task was to understand whether or not the customer had received our on-site training in how to stop the appliance vibrating at the wrong time. It turned out that she was unaware of this training service, but indicated that she was willing to try the training before returning the appliance.
Action	So I organised for our trainers to visit her later the very same day.
Result	The result was her appliance stopped slipping and she wrote to us in praise of our helpful and prompt service.
Point forward	I will always take time to find out the background to a customer's complaint because it's much easier to work out what will turn them into a satisfied customer again.

A story for every occasion

So now you know how to structure the stories, the next thing to do is to develop a range of stories that illustrates your achievements for each competency you have identified as important during your job detective work. It helps when working this out to use a form of mind mapping to set out each competency and the stories that relate to it. To do this, we need to follow a three-step process:

1 Write the name of the competency in the middle of a blank sheet of paper.

2 Now think of concrete (key) examples of *behaviour* in your role that are relevant to both the competency *and* the role you are applying for.

3 Finally, write a PREP-STAR story for each identified key behaviour.

The result might look like Figure 12.1. (Here we have written only two stories, obviously you would generate a story for each key behaviour.)

Putting it all together

So now you have around four or more detailed stories, all set out in the PREP-STAR formula, ready-made to slot into your competency statements. Your only problem is to decide which of the stories to select. Your selections should be guided by the model of fit, and therefore you should choose the strongest stories that best enhance the fit between you and the job.

The other stories are not wasted though: these can be kept in reserve for use in the interview. Imagine how you would feel going into the interview and being able to respond to a question such as 'Can you tell us about your communication skills' and you can reply, 'Well, do you want me to expand on the examples I gave on the CV regarding writing memorable ads and creatively resolving disputes, or would you like me to tell you about my public speaking and listening skills?' You will feel a million dollars, because you have all these convincing stories at your fingertips and will be able to go beyond the CV, so proving you are not a one-trick pony with only one tale to tell!

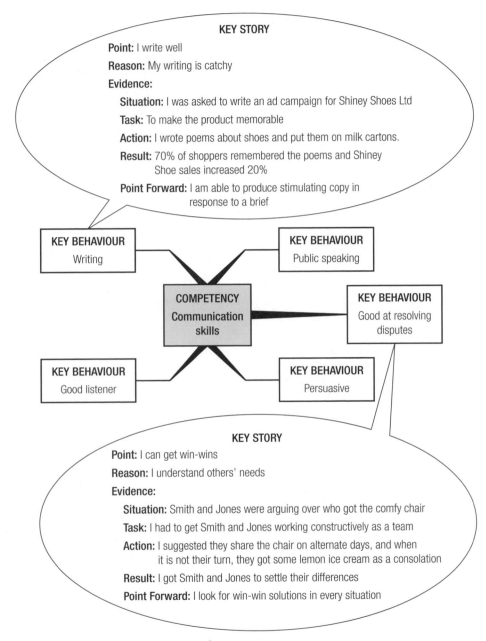

KEY STORY

Point: I write well

Reason: My writing is catchy

Evidence:

    Situation: I was asked to write an ad campaign for Shiney Shoes Ltd

    Task: To make the product memorable

    Action: I wrote poems about shoes and put them on milk cartons.

    Result: 70% of shoppers remembered the poems and Shiney
            Shoe sales increased 20%

    Point Forward: I am able to produce stimulating copy in
                  response to a brief

KEY BEHAVIOUR
Writing

KEY BEHAVIOUR
Public speaking

COMPETENCY
Communication skills

KEY BEHAVIOUR
Good at resolving disputes

KEY BEHAVIOUR
Good listener

KEY BEHAVIOUR
Persuasive

KEY STORY

Point: I can get win-wins

Reason: I understand others' needs

Evidence:

    Situation: Smith and Jones were arguing over who got the comfy chair

    Task: I had to get Smith and Jones working constructively as a team

    Action: I suggested they share the chair on alternate days, and when
            it is not their turn, they got some lemon ice cream as a consolation

    Result: I got Smith and Jones to settle their differences

    Point Forward: I look for win-win solutions in every situation

Figure 12.1 Mind-mapping stories for a competency

A word about length

Remember what we said about the 'fit' model in Chapter 2. If the CV becomes too long and boring it will reduce the fit between you and the job. However, there are no set rules about length, other than the general guideline that if something increases the fit between you and the job, include the information on the CV. If it reduces the fit, do not include it. If pressed for a rule-of-thumb guideline, most people can say what needs to be said in two or three pages, and most senior people can do it in around five pages.

Some research suggests that there might be variations across different industries. For example, 39 per cent of recruiters surveyed in the recreation and leisure service industry preferred a CV of between two and four pages long[1]. Most recruiters emphasise the importance of tailoring content to match the industry's specific requirements and avoiding a 'one size fits all' approach to résumé writing. Start with a two to three page CV as a guide and then see what types of questions you are asked at interview to determine the areas to expand on.

A worked example of a PREP-STAR résumé

David Brent

42 Paper Lace Parade	Telephone: (0191) 667 1111
Slough	Fax: (0191) 667 1112
Email: brentd@HeliInc.com	Mobile: (07733) 123456

Career objective

To secure a busy 'hands-on' senior financial role that provides challenge and capitalises on my accounting expertise. I am keen to find a position closer to home so that I can combine professional with personal fulfilment.
Skills, experience and personal attributes

---

[1] Ross, C. M. and Young, S. J. (2005). 'Resume preferences: Is it really business as usual?' *Journal of Career Development*, 32(2), 153–164.

Accounting expertise

Having a varied finance background in both the public and private sector, I feel confident in my ability to fulfil the role of financial accountant as outlined. My experience in the taxation office has provided me with a thorough understanding of financial reporting requirements.

Last financial year at Helicopters Inc. I overhauled the taxation and general ledger processes. I reviewed and revised all the financial reporting mechanisms within the company, leading to a 10% reduction in the time taken to produce reports, and I received a commendation from the board for the clarity and accuracy of our reports. This outcome reflects how I use my advanced accounting knowledge to bring about concrete benefits to my employer.

Attention to detail

Attention to detail is an essential performance criterion in my current role at Helicopters Inc. and I pride myself on achieving excellence in this area. For instance, I compile a monthly report to management on the key financial drivers within the business, based on a range of company and economic statistics. I have set up a process where the relevant information is sent to me throughout the reporting period and incorporated into the report on an on-going basis. It is then triple checked before final distribution so that all reports are delivered on time and with no errors. When information is used to make critical business decisions, I always ensure that it is accurate.

Ability to manage multiple tasks

I regularly need to work towards numerous and competing deadlines. In June four separate important deadlines fell within one week. To meet these deadlines, I identified time-consuming tasks I could delegate to four team members which enabled me to focus on items which required my higher-level input. We met all the deadlines with time to spare, and we achieved the best possible result for the company. When confronted with a demanding workload I will always keep a cool head and determine the most efficient approach to get the job done.

Education

2002–2005 Bachelor of Commerce (Accounting) University of Sunderland

Memberships

2007 Member, Institute of Chartered Accountants
2014 Member, Institute of Company Directors

Employment history

Financial Controller   Helicopters Inc., Middlesbrough

Dec. 2010 – current

Responsibilities

Preparation, consolidation and review of management and project
reporting, overseeing the preparation of progress claims and analysis
and reporting on cashflow, controlling and covering all foreign exchange
exposures, ensuring that all insurance requirements for the project and
contract are met, liaison with banks for provision of security required under
the contracts and sub-contracts, supervision of two accounting staff.

Achievements

- Implemented new project reporting system to suit management team needs
- Met all management reporting deadlines
- Reduced time spent on compiling information in department by 65%
- Substituted for company secretary in his absence.

Assistant Financial Controller   Helicopters Inc., Middlesbrough

Feb. 2006 – Nov. 2010

Responsibilities

Consolidation and preparation of management and statutory accounts,
tax returns and budgets, review and analysis of operating results for
senior management, overseeing the preparation of monthly board reports,
developing and implementing foreign exchange trading procedures and
systems, review and support of capital expenditure proposals.

Achievements

- Implemented new foreign exchange trading procedures and systems
- All reporting deadlines met.

Referees

Mr Fred Scuttle
Managing Director, Helicopters Inc.
(01642) 991234

Mr Robert Todd
Chairman, Helicopters Inc
(01642) 991230

But wait, there's more, CAROL!

Here is another very useful formula for organising the information in your competency statements – the CAROL formula. Check out our résumé makeovers and you'll see us employing PREP-STAR and CAROL throughout. Charles Dickens' *A Christmas Carol* is a great story, and you can write a CV Carol to write yourself to success.

Context	Just enough essential background information so that the reader can understand your actions.
Actions	What you did and how you did it, concentrating on descriptive action verbs so that the reader can imagine you in action.
Reasons	Why you did what you did to show that your actions were deliberate rather than just lucky guesses.
Outcomes	What you achieved and how successful your actions were to show how good you are.
Learning	What the reader can infer about your future actions and usefulness from this story.

 **example**

Context	Two weeks ago I had a customer come into our store who was complaining that her appliance had slipped.
Actions & Reasons*	*Because she was quite upset*, I initially concentrated on listening and acknowledging her complaint. When she had calmed down, I encouraged her to describe how she had been using her appliance, *to work out whether she had been using it incorrectly*. I discovered that she had not received any training. *As an alternative to a refund*, I offered to organise priority training free of charge and she agreed.
Outcomes	After the training she was able to use the appliance without further difficulty and she wrote a letter praising my helpfulness and support.
Learning	I have found that making an effort to understand the customer and their reasons for dissatisfaction increases my ability to find mutually beneficial solutions to their problems.

*Reason statements in italic.

brilliant **example**

David Brent CV

Accounting expertise

Last financial year at Helicopters Inc. I overhauled the taxation and general ledger processes. Having observed a number of inefficiencies, I reviewed and revised all the financial reporting mechanisms. By surveying senior management about their reporting needs I was able to streamline the report structures. This change led to a 10% reduction in the time taken to produce reports and a commendation from the board for the clarity and accuracy of our reports. From this experience I learnt the importance of questioning existing processes and gaining a greater understanding of stakeholder needs.

Attention to detail

Attention to detail is an essential performance criterion in my current role and I regularly achieve excellent ratings in this area. For instance, I compile a monthly report to management on key financial business drivers, based on company and economic statistics. To ensure I have the information available when I need it I have established a process where relevant data is incorporated into a draft report on an on-going basis. It is then triple checked before final distribution so that all reports are delivered on time and with no errors. When information is used to make critical business decisions, I always ensure that it is accurate.

Ability to manage multiple tasks

I regularly need to work towards numerous and competing deadlines. In June four separate important deadlines fell within one week. To prioritise effectively, I identified potentially time-consuming tasks I could delegate to four team members. This enabled me to focus on items which required my higher-level input. We met all the deadlines with time to spare, and we achieved the best possible result for the company. When faced with multiple tasks I take a strategic approach to prioritising and planning in order to increase efficiency.

CHAPTER 13

Using career objectives

What is a career objective statement?

A recent trend has been to include a career objective at the beginning of your CV. The career objective is a succinct statement that describes what you want out of a job. It allows the reader to get a quick idea of your suitability for the job advertised, and it also serves to make you appear more motivated.

Career objectives can be as simple as stating what sort of job you are looking for. For instance someone in the medical world might write:

Employment in a hospital specialising in care of the elderly.

These sorts of statements have their uses in letting the reader know quickly whether you are a serious contender for the job. However, if the person in the above example would also be happy caring for young children, they may be narrowing their opportunities unnecessarily. Such statements might also be seen by the reader as rather obvious. (After all, they have applied for the job!)

A good career statement might read:

Accounts manager in a growing organisation, where I can use my communication skills to deal with a variety of clients.

The statement is positive, it doesn't sound too desperate, in the way that a statement like 'To work for your organisation' does, and it is not too limited.

A bad career statement starts:

All I've ever wanted to be is …

The statement above is a real example, and gives the impression of very limited ambition and narrow focus.

It is sometimes better to see the career objective as an opportunity to market yourself as well as stating what you want to do. The example below shows how you can slip in some positive comments about your skill levels and motivation.

▶ brilliant example

A position as training manager in a progressive multinational company where I can maximise the use of my communication and teaching skills and where I will be continually challenged and stretched.

Do they work?

A lot of people get terribly self-conscious about using these sorts of statements. However, in a study we did with recruiters, we found that CVs that included career objectives influenced recruiters to think the applicants were more suited to the job they had applied for. So, yes, they do work and you should consider including one on your CV.

Career objectives probably become less effective the more experienced you are. They are certainly a good idea for young applicants, graduates and people in the first five or so years of their working career. They may also be a good option for people looking at changing careers.

As the name implies, they should be statements about your desired career, so they are not really appropriate for temporary jobs such as student vacation jobs. 'To develop my skills in waiting on tables …' doesn't sound quite right.

CHAPTER 14

Job application
letters

What is a covering letter for?

All CVs should be accompanied by a covering letter. The covering letter has several purposes:

- it lets administrative staff know quickly what the correspondence is about
- it is often the first thing an employer reads
- it allows you to say why you are applying
- it sets the tone for the CV.

Many authors seem to suggest you produce fairly standard CVs and put your efforts into tailoring the covering letter. We do not think this is the best approach, and it should be clear that we believe you should tailor the CV for each job. One very sound reason for this is that it is the CV that usually gets more attention, and generally it is the CV that is used as the basis of questions asked in employment interviews (not the covering letter).

Covering letters should be taken seriously. However, do not think that a 'one size fits all' approach to your CV can be compensated for by a covering letter.

Application letter rules

Here are the basic guidelines for writing a letter of application for a job:

- you must write a new one for each application
- the addressee must be correct – do not cut and paste letters
- the date must be correct
- they should never be more than one page long
- they should be as well laid out as your CV
- unless a handwritten response is specifically asked for, you should type your letters.

brilliant tip

Do not state information in the covering letter that can be obtained from reading your CV.

Your letter should include the following information:

- your (typed) name, address, email address and phone number (with area code)
- the name of the person to whom you are writing (get this from the job advertisement, or phone the company and ask to whom you should address the letter)
- their job title
- their address
- the initial greeting (for example, 'Dear Ms Smith,' or 'Dear Sir,')
- the first sentence, which should state:
  - the job you are applying for
  - reference number
  - where you saw the post advertised
- a couple of sentences that are catchy statements such as those we developed as competency statements (Chapter 11). ('I have over five years' experience as a machinist with Bloggs and Bloggs, and have experience of a wide variety of pattern techniques.')
- a couple of sentences about why this employer/job is right for you

- a polite request for a reply
- your signature and your name typed below it.

The following example will give you a guide.

Sample covering letter

Jenny Halse
15 Castle Street
Guildford, Surrey
GU3 2PS
Tel: (01483) 2934532
20 July 2013

Robert Wayne
Fabrication Manager
Laughing Boy Dog Toys
2 Railway Cuttings
East Cheam, Surrey
CR7 2OT

Dear Mr Wayne

I wish to apply for the position of machinist (ref 301/13) that was advertised in the *Evening Standard* on Saturday, 20 July 2013.

I have over five years' experience as a Machinist with Weaveanduck and have knowledge of a wide variety of pattern techniques. My technical skills are second to none, and I have an excellent record as a reliable, productive employee.

I am looking for new challenges and the position of Machinist sounds the perfect opportunity. Your organisation has an enviable record in innovation in machining, and an excellent reputation as an employer, making the position even more attractive.

I enclose my CV for your consideration and look forward to hearing from you soon. I am available for interview at your convenience.

Yours sincerely

Jenny Halse

PART 3

The doctor is in – your problems solved

At this stage you have put together a strong CV, and you have given it a shine and extra polish, but still there are those nagging questions about particular aspects of the document. This section will answer those questions for you.

Also included are some sample CVs for you to look at in relation to the earlier chapters. We would emphasise, though, that we believe you should tailor your own CV to each specific job, so while we hope these examples give you some ideas and inspiration, it is not our goal for you just to copy them. We hope that if you have read the book up to this point you are persuaded by the scientific evidence and the feedback from recruiters that tailoring your own résumé provides you with the best chance of producing a CV that gets short-listed. Good luck in your job hunting.

CHAPTER 15

Addressing
selection criteria

Selection criteria are a list of written job requirements that candidates must demonstrate they meet before being short-listed. Selection criteria are really important and should not be confused with the usual hyperbole found in most job advertisements. They are extremely common, and often mandatory across most public sector jobs including local and national government, education and other positions in the public realm. Failure to explicitly and fully address selection criteria can (and very often will) lead to automatic rejection, no matter what your individual merits may be. As we said, they are important and need to be taken seriously.

Selection criteria are statements that set out fairly precisely the sorts of qualities, experience, training and behaviours (in other words, the knowledge, skills, abilities and attitudes) that the employer seeks for the position. Employers believe that these statements help them sort out the strong candidates from the weak. Furthermore, they are supposed to encourage employers to rank applicants based only on job-relevant criteria and therefore reduce prejudice and bias that come from employers making judgements about a candidate's race, gender, age, attractiveness, etc.

Here's the good news. What we've talked about in relation to analysing job ads and writing competency statements will come in very handy in addressing selection criteria.

Deciphering the selection criteria

These are the most common parts of the selection criteria statements:

- **Competency**: This is a work-related attribute much like competency statements (Chapter 11). This includes things like communication skills, teamwork, leadership, ability to meet deadlines.

- **Qualifier**: This sets the level of performance a company requires and puts boundaries on what they are asking for, for instance, whether they want 'advanced' accounting knowledge, or merely an 'appreciation' of accounting practices. Other terms are commonly used, such as 'superior', 'excellent', 'outstanding', 'strong', 'demonstrated', 'background in', 'experience of', 'ability to', 'understanding of'.

- **Behaviour**: This usually puts into context where and how the competency has to be demonstrated.

- **Importance**: There are sometimes two main categories: essential and desirable. 'Essential' means that you must demonstrate that you meet this criterion to be short-listed. No manner of excuses or obfuscation will get you around a failure to address essential criteria.

- **Desirable**: This does not mean these criteria are the most important, rather the opposite. It means that failure to address this criterion will not automatically lead to rejection, but candidates who can demonstrate they meet the desirable criteria are likely to be ranked higher and more likely to be short-listed. Always try to demonstrate that you possess the desirable criteria where possible.

Not all statements will include all these components. For instance, some statements will not refer directly to behaviour, others might not include the qualifier, etc.

Here is a typical set of criteria dissected into their components.

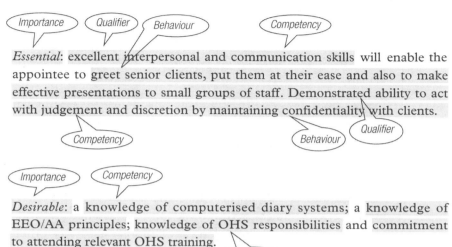

Decoding the jargon – competencies

The competencies contained in most selection criteria are usually the same as those found in general job ads (teamwork, leadership, communication skills, attention to detail, etc.). (See Chapter 11 for details of the most common competency statements and what they mean.)

Some competency statements elevate jargon to a more prominent role, which you cannot ignore. Common examples here include: knowledge of EEO/AA principles, knowledge of OHS policies and responsibilities, and advanced computer literacy. The first two examples refer to the organisation's policies in respect of equal employment opportunities, affirmative action and occupational health and safety. The last example calls for a high level of familiarity and skill using a range of software programs. Generally, 'advanced' computer skills would mean you can use all of the basic Office 'productivity' software such as Microsoft Word (word processor), Excel (spreadsheet), Outlook (email), Explorer (Web browser). In addition you would be expected to use these programs to a high level (e.g. you could write programs in the spreadsheet to calculate numbers) and/or be able to use a range of other programs like PowerPoint, Access or specialist software related to their business like accounts, payroll or design software.

How do I know whether the company is asking about competencies or selection criteria?

Sometimes employers will be obvious about the fact that they want you to address selection criteria. You will see job advertisements with statements like 'Applicants are required to obtain the full selection criteria from the recruitment website at: **www.recruithere.com**' or 'Selection documentation can be obtained by ringing the Defence Service Centre' or 'Selection criteria and details on how to apply can be found on the Laughing Dog website **www.hadoggyha.co.uk**'. In this instance you will usually be provided with details about length of the CV and any other requirements. At other times, it is not so obvious. If an advertisement uses the headings 'Essential and Desirable Criteria' and there are more than six points in total, you should treat the advertisement as if a separate attachment is required for selection criteria (see below).

Decoding the jargon – qualifiers

Outstanding, superior, excellent, strong, sound

These are the normal hyperbolic words that we have come to know and love! Do not be intimidated by them. It means you are reasonably good at something. For instance, the fact that you have the capacity for thought, language and creativity (sometimes at the same time) sets you apart from Jim's Welsh Springer Spaniels and therefore you possess superior, outstanding, excellent, strong and sound skills. Note these statements rarely state against what standard they are making the judgements of excellence, superiority, etc. Do not be put off using such positive descriptors to describe your own talents.

Knowledge of, understanding of

At the very least you've got to demonstrate you know what they are talking about! So 'knowledge of wireless networking' might get a response mentioning the names of network programs you have used, or the names of network hardware. You might be able to get away with 'I have knowledge of wireless networking appropriate to the requirements of this position' if you are really desperate and have only slight knowledge of the programs, but are confident you could learn about them. Remember that whatever you claim may be more closely examined in an interview, so be honest and make sure you are not stretching the truth.

Demonstrate your knowledge with evidence wherever you can. So the reply might be 'I have knowledge of wireless networks, having installed an IEEE 802.11b-compliant PCMCIA Type-II 11Mbps wireless LAN adapter in my current job'. (*Note*: an IEEE 802.11b-compliant PCMCIA Type-II 11Mbps wireless LAN adapter is a very mysterious thing and should not be talked about in polite company!)

Demonstrated ability to

This means you are actually required to provide evidence in your statements that you have done this thing. For instance, demonstrated ability to exercise taste and judgement in editing the company newsletter could be addressed with: 'As editor of the Departmental Circular, I had to take the decision to remove a humorous article submitted by a junior and excitable employee. The article had the capacity to cause offence to those who did not get the joke and, as the primary goal of the publication was to inform and assist, as opposed to entertain, I was able to convince my colleague to resubmit the article with the jokes removed. I was praised on the quality of the publication under my editorship and received no complaints from the readership.'

Background in, experience of

This means the company is looking for evidence that you have done the tasks or acquired the competency in the past, preferably in your current or previous jobs. Generally this refers to work you've done, more than training you've completed. So emphasise work experience first and foremost, but do not omit relevant training if space permits.

Appreciation of

This usually means that you've heard of something, or there is a possibility that the position will have some relation to whatever the advertisement is asking about. It normally does not signify the central or crucial knowledge, skills and abilities in the job. Often it is used in relation to policies like equal employment opportunities. You do not have to be an expert in employment policies, but appreciate that they exist, and understand in broad terms what they mean.

Steps in addressing selection criteria

1   Create a document that is separate from your CV.

2   Title this document 'Statements addressing the selection criteria' (or use the phrase the employer uses in the advertisement, such as 'Statement of claim for the position').

3   Use each of the selection criteria as headings.

4   Address each criterion carefully, providing evidence to back up your claims.

5   Ensure you have addressed all aspects of each selection criterion.

6   Draw upon different evidence in support of different criteria (i.e. do not repeat the same achievements over and over for each criterion).

7   Use positive and unequivocal language. Avoid using qualifiers like 'quite good', or 'some', 'a little', 'reasonable', 'average'.

8   Use your job detective skills to ensure you understand what each of the criteria means (see Chapter 3).

9   Check for word limit (some employers stipulate total number of pages allowable for the selection criteria). If there is no word limit indicated, then assume it is fine to write about half a page of A4 paper's worth of text. Yes! One or two sentences are generally not going to be sufficient. On the other hand, given that there are generally five or more statements to address, if you write much more than half a page you run the risk of boring the reader and hence not being short-listed.

10 Make sure every claim you make in addressing these statements is consistent with any claims, achievements or job history contained in your CV.

How does this affect the style and content of my CV?

Many employers will ask you to address the selection criteria in a separate document and also send in a CV. Now the issue arises of what to include in the CV and what to include in the selection criteria. The answer to this dilemma is that you must always fully address the selection criteria in the explicit statement headed 'Addressing the selection criteria' because this is the single most crucial document in the decision-making process. However, that does not mean you should slack off on the CV, or that you need not include competency statements on the CV.

Clearly you will have dealt with many of the competencies that you normally would have included in the CV while addressing the selection criteria. However, there may well be some that have not been included in the selection criteria that you could include to good effect on the CV – for instance, attention to detail, tenacity and numeracy, to name a few. Including additional competency statements even if they are not requested impresses recruiters. Evidence Jim Bright published in an international selection journal with Sonia Manser shows that CVs that included extra competency statements over and above the required ones were rated even more highly than CVs that exactly addressed the competency statements. (*Note*: do not include additional statements on your separate document entitled 'Addressing the selection criteria' – this document must address exactly what the employers are asking for.)

If all your competencies are fully covered in the separate document, then it is still worth considering including highly abridged (succinct) statements on three or four of the most relevant competencies. However, keep these to no more than one or two bullets or sentences. This will allow your CV to stand alone from the selection criteria document, but will not be overly repetitious.

Sometimes the candidate is asked to address the selection criteria in the covering letter. Do not fall into the trap that many do, of providing overly succinct, breezy or casual statements in the belief that the covering letter needs to be short. Normally you would be correct in keeping the covering letter short, but in this case you have been invited to write a much longer one.

We recommend that the first page of the letter follows the template in Chapter 14. Include a statement towards the end of the letter saying 'There follows after this page a statement explicitly addressing the job criteria. I have also included my CV for your consideration.' Then attach your statements addressing the job criteria and remember to include your CV!

Let's look at an example from the criteria we listed earlier.

brilliant example

Knowledge of OHS responsibilities and commitment to attend relevant OHS training

I am an employee-elected representative of our Workplace Safety Committee at Blue Blot Inc. In this capacity I am required to have a knowledge of our Occupational Health and Safety requirements from a legislative point of view as well as recognising that best safety practice makes good business sense. I have completed the training course 'Workplace Committees' accredited by the HSE. This was a four-day course. I also self-initiated and completed the two-day course 'Workplace First Aid Level 2'. I have been called upon to provide first aid to other employees, and to ensure that any accidents that occur are appropriately recorded. One accident involving faulty printing equipment required investigation by the HSE. I assisted the HSE in their investigations, by organising interviews with the appropriate parties, providing technical information in relation to the equipment (such as maintenance records) and ensuring access to the offending equipment. The HSE cleared Blue Blot Inc. of any responsibility for the accident, and the equipment used by us has since been recalled by the manufacturer. This was considered a good outcome for Blue Blot Inc. since the alternative may have been a complete shut-down of our business. Our OHS committee meets monthly, and I am required to regularly review our OHS policies, discuss near-misses, evaluate preventative measures or solutions, and identify possible training needs and courses. In my capacity as Blue Blot Inc.'s receptionist I am required to ensure that any on-site contractors provide evidence of having completed relevant safety training and certification before beginning work.

Put the work in to get the work

Selection criteria can be intimidating for people who have not had to write this sort of material before. Even very experienced and educated people can be reduced to a nervous wreck when confronted by these requests. Put aside plenty of time to write them. Seriously consider getting professional help. Always have a friend, partner or, better still, a colleague read and critique them. Always ask the question, 'Have I provided a convincing argument that directly and clearly addresses the job criteria?' Be prepared to write and rewrite this section. It is the single most important section in many job application processes and may well influence what the recruiting panel decide to ask you about during the interview. It is tragically the case that all of the authors of this book have sat on panels where candidates we know to be excellent are rejected out of hand because they have failed to meet the selection criteria. It is a matter of procedural fairness in some organisations, so never believe that you are so well regarded that you can afford to ignore this section.

CHAPTER 16

CV makeovers

I n the following examples, some of the original CVs are poor due to layout and formatting but contain good information. The examples of 'before' CVs are typical of the ones we receive at Bright and Associates from clients wanting professional rewrites. We think that every CV for each person and each job should be crafted carefully, so what we present is not designed to be copied slavishly; rather, we use them to illustrate how our principles of CV writing can be applied. The job advertisement for the CV is included too, so that you can see how to address the points in the advertisement. For each career stage, the key points to bear in mind are set out so that you can make sure you have addressed them when you write your CV.

School leaver

It can be a challenge to stand out from the crowd as you'll have had fewer opportunities to gain the same experience as older job seekers. Generally, we advise people to omit hobbies and interests from their CV, but we make an exception for school leavers as this section may contain evidence of your maturity, community mindedness, team abilities, and so on. School leavers need to focus on layout, grammar, attention to detail, and addressing the selection criteria. Do not try to claim significant experience unless you truly have it, because at this stage you are selling yourself on promise rather than past events. Nobody will expect a school leaver to have had years of job-relevant experience, and, unless such claims are supported by convincing evidence, you run the risk of recruiters dismissing you as a liar, deluded, or hopelessly out of touch with what experience really means.

Here is an example of a job advertisement relevant to a school leaver.

ADMINISTRATION ASSISTANT

Due to expansion, an exciting opportunity exists for a person to assist the Administration Manager in a wide variety of work such as marketing mail-outs, customer relations and all other aspects of administration.

Applicants must possess good communication skills with the ability to work under pressure during peak work load times. Knowledge of Word and Excel essential. Package negotiable.

Send CV to:

Human Resources Director, Lords Insurance Brokers, PO Box 111, St John's Wood, London N2.

The 'before' CV

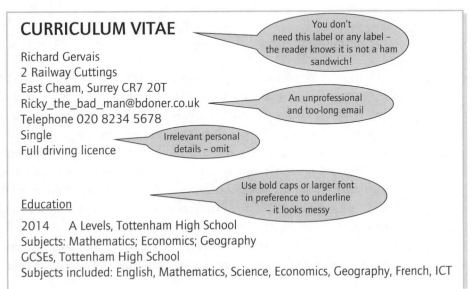

CURRICULUM VITAE

You don't need this label or any label – the reader knows it is not a ham sandwich!

Richard Gervais
2 Railway Cuttings
East Cheam, Surrey CR7 2OT
Ricky_the_bad_man@bdoner.co.uk
Telephone 020 8234 5678
Single
Full driving licence

An unprofessional and too-long email

Irrelevant personal details – omit

Use bold caps or larger font in preference to underline – it looks messy

Education

2014   A Levels, Tottenham High School
Subjects: Mathematics; Economics; Geography
GCSEs, Tottenham High School
Subjects included: English, Mathematics, Science, Economics, Geography, French, ICT

Work history

Feb 2013 – Dec 2014   Secretary, Interact Club, Tottenham High School
Feb 2013 – Dec 2014   Service Assistant (part-time), Harvey Norman,
                       Oxford St, London

Where are duties, achievements?

Interests and activities

Meeting new people, computing, public speaking, regular blood donor
Feb 2011 – Dec 2014 Interact Club
I am keen to learn, hardworking and good with computers. I have an excellent attitude.

References

Mr Sidney James   Mr Kenneth Williams
Manager, Harvey Norman   Head Teacher, Tottenham High School
020 8122 3333   020 8919 1567

This candidate is not selling himself. What about personal qualities and addressing the selection criteria?

The 'after' CV

This CV is much more accomplished. It is much better set out and space is not wasted on silly column structures. The key competencies clearly address the selection criteria mentioned in the job. The CV emphasises achievements all the way through. Jobs and schooling are clearly explained, highlighting what was done well.

Richard Gervais

Address: 2 Railway Cuttings   Telephone: (020) 8234 5678
East Cheam, Surrey CR7 2OT   Email address: r.gervais@it.co.uk

Career objective

I am looking for a busy, entry-level position in administration that utilises my computing and organisational skills while enabling me to learn about a business from the ground up.

Skills, experience and personal attributes

Communication skills

I have been developing my public speaking skills while competing in the Rostrum public speaking competitions. This experience has given me the confidence to express myself clearly and confidently. As a finalist in the Rostrum public speaking competition I was invited to present to no fewer than 200 people. I regularly use my written communication skills in the composing of correspondence and promotional material for the Interact Club.

Customer relations skills

While at Harvey Norman, I have helped many customers, resulting in my being awarded 'Employee of the Month' five times. I take time to listen to customers, identify their needs and then recommend products that are most suitable. While at Harvey Norman I have attended a two-day training course on Customer Service Skills.

Time management skills

While completing my A Levels I have held down a part-time position at Harvey Norman as well as being Secretary to the Interact Club. These extra-curricular activities have put additional demands on my time, and without careful planning my school work would have suffered. I have never missed a school deadline or needed an extension to complete work. To make the best use of my time I schedule it and complete tasks in order of priority. I believe these time management skills will transfer well to the workplace.

Computer skills

During my ICT (Computing) GCSE I became familiar with a number of office software packages including Excel, Word, PowerPoint and Access as well as common e-mail programs such as Outlook and Thunderbird. I have used Word to produce flyers and promotional mailings for the Interact club and have used Dreamweaver to edit the club webpages.

Education

Secondary

2014   A Levels, Tottenham High School
2012   Subjects: Mathematics; Economics; Geography
            GCSEs, Tottenham High School
            Subjects included: English, Mathematics, Science, Economics,
            Geography, French, ICT

Other courses

2013–2014   Customer Service Skills, In-House Harvey Norman

Academic achievements

Nov 2014   Ranked top student in Economics at Tottenham High School
Nov 2014   Rostrum Public Speaking Competition Finalist

Employment history

Feb 2013–Dec 2014   Secretary, Interact Club, Tottenham High School

Duties included:

- taking and typing up minutes of weekly meetings; composing and typing outgoing correspondence
- organising mail-outs to students on club activities; prioritising and acting on in-coming correspondence; editing the club's webpages.

Achievements:

- awarded with school prize for community involvement
- membership increased from 10 to 17 members following mailings that I initiated
- all in-coming mail dealt with within seven days of receipt.

Feb 2013–Dec 2014 Service Assistant (part-time), Harvey Norman, Oxford Street

Duties included:

- helping customers with location of products; explaining different features of products to customers
- dealing with customer complaints when products returned
- serving customers at cash registers and stocking shelves with products.

Achievements:

- 'Employee of the Month' May 2013, Nov 2013, Feb 2014, July 2014, Sep 2014 (based on customer nomination)
- awarded Employee with 'Best knowledge – bathroom fittings' by Caroma (supplier).

Interests and activities

Meeting new people, computing, public speaking, regular blood donor
Feb 2013–Dec 2014 Interact Club

Referees

Mr Sidney James
Manager, Harvey Norman
(020) 8222 3333

Mr Kenneth Williams
Head Teacher, Tottenham High School
(020) 8919 1567

School leaver checklist

The following checklist will provide you with a quick reminder of all the key things you need for your CV:

- Name, full address, telephone numbers, up-to-date email address that
- reflects the image you want to portray
- Full details of any relevant experience whether paid or voluntary
- Full educational qualifications
- Details of any interests or hobbies
- Emphasis on achievements and results
- Believable competency statements backed up with evidence
- A snappy career statement
- Printed on high-quality paper or e-mailed as a PDF
- Two referees (whom you have already approached), including their full contact details

Graduates

Graduates have several challenges. First, if you have not worked whilst at university you face similar issues to a school leaver and it might be worth checking out the previous section. Graduates can make a couple of basic mistakes. They can assume that their degree has given them all of the experience they will need to be successful in the graduate job market and in the workplace. Many graduate recruiters in the UK are less interested in the knowledge and expertise you have gained in your subject and more concerned with your ability to apply your thinking skills to real-world problems at work. For them a good degree result is a baseline, not the be all and end all. On the other hand, many students fail to identify the skills that they have developed during their time at university that could be relevant to a number of different graduate roles.

Employers are increasingly interested in well-rounded applicants and, while high academic achievement is clearly desirable, they will be looking for evidence that you have made the most of all the opportunities afforded you at university. So getting involved in clubs and societies, or giving something back to the community through voluntary or charitable work, will be well received. Leadership skills, teamwork, presentation skills, and so on, can all be gained by getting involved in extra-curricular activities. These demonstrate to an employer that you are well-rounded as a person and have taken a strategic approach to getting the right competencies.

Graduates are about the only group of people that have employers targeting them specifically for special recruitment schemes, and you should realise that many of the larger organisations will start their recruitment schemes early in your final year. On top of that, many of the big graduate recruiters fill places on their permanent schemes with students who secured internships with them in their penultimate year. So you have to be thinking about work earlier than you may have expected.

The following is a job advertisement directed at graduates.

GRADUATE ENGINEER

ASM Power is setting a dynamic pace in the UK standby power market.

Our current Operations and Engineering Managers joined as graduates, and their rapid progression creates openings for new graduates.

A structured two-year development programme will help you master a broad engineering/operations/management role. Commitment and enthusiasm will be required as you become involved in Production/Capacity Planning, Purchasing, Customer Liaison, Personnel Management, Process Re-Engineering and Supplier Negotiations.

You will need confident speaking and presentation skills, high computer literacy, and a willingness to embrace new ideas.

Above all, you will recognise a great opportunity.

Send applications by 5th June to: David Bradshaw HR Director, ASM Power, New Industrial Estate, Croydon CO1 1MU

The 'before' CV

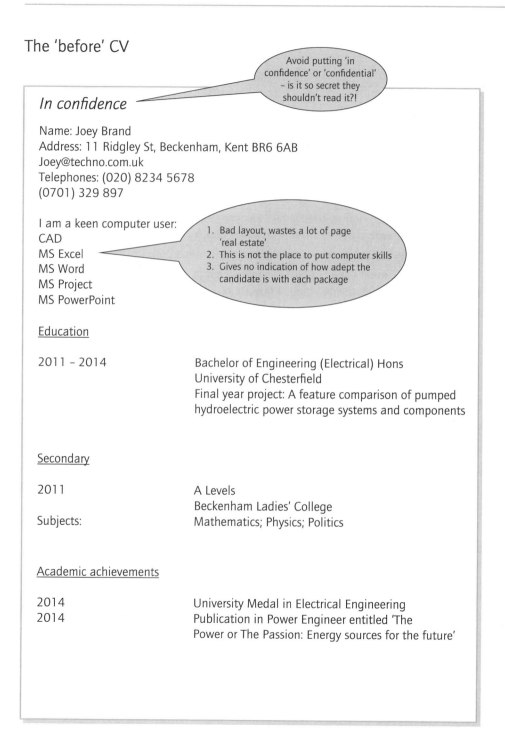

Avoid putting 'in confidence' or 'confidential' – is it so secret they shouldn't read it?!

In confidence

Name: Joey Brand
Address: 11 Ridgley St, Beckenham, Kent BR6 6AB
Joey@techno.com.uk
Telephones: (020) 8234 5678
(0701) 329 897

I am a keen computer user:
CAD
MS Excel
MS Word
MS Project
MS PowerPoint

1. Bad layout, wastes a lot of page 'real estate'
2. This is not the place to put computer skills
3. Gives no indication of how adept the candidate is with each package

Education

2011 – 2014   Bachelor of Engineering (Electrical) Hons
                   University of Chesterfield
                   Final year project: A feature comparison of pumped
                   hydroelectric power storage systems and components

Secondary

2011   A Levels
                   Beckenham Ladies' College
Subjects: Mathematics; Physics; Politics

Academic achievements

2014   University Medal in Electrical Engineering
2014   Publication in Power Engineer entitled 'The
                   Power or The Passion: Energy sources for the future'

Employment history

July 2013 – Sept 2013 Associate Electrical Engineer

Summer Internship, Somercotes Power Station, Alfreton

Responsibilities

- assist electrical engineer in the design and layout of electrical installations and circuitry
- collect information, perform complex calculations and prepare diagrams and drawings of electrical installations and circuitry
- use CAD to produce designs and detailed drawings
- assist in testing and commissioning of electrical equipment and installations, and in the supervision of operations and maintenance.

Interests and activities

University debating team, computer simulations, personal computing, cooking, hockey. My final year research project, 'A feature comparison of pumped hydroelectric power storage systems and components', looked at the various components and system configurations for hydroelectric power storage.

Referees

Mr Eric Sykes
(01773) 239777

Prof. James Edwards
UoC (01246) 114678

> Ragged and poor formatting, especially the small bullets and the second line of each bullet – learn how to use a word processor or find someone who knows how to use one!

> No reference to achievements, just a list of duties performed. It looks like a lot of 'helping out'

> This repeats information already provided on the front page

> Doesn't say what positions these people hold, they could just be mates!

> Complete failure to address the key job requirements as set out in the ad

The 'after' CV

This CV sets out all of the information in a much more logical manner. The selection criteria are explicitly addressed. Redundant information such as 'In confidence' and 'Name:' are removed. Achievements are highlighted, and the layout is significantly improved.

Josephine Brand

Address: 11 Ridgley St, Beckenham, Kent BR6 6AB

Telephone: (020) 8234 5678

Email address: J.Brand@techno.co.uk   Mobile: 07011 329897

Career objective

I am keen to launch a career in electrical engineering within the power industry to further develop and utilise my high levels of computer literacy and confident presentation skills. The organisation I am seeking is progressive and able to provide a comprehensive and structured learning programme, such as offered by ASM Power.

Skills, experience and personal attributes

Speaking and presentation skills

I am a confident and articulate public speaker. I was a finalist at the National University debating challenge held in Oxford last year. In addition to this I have presented to challenging academic panels on my university honours thesis. While at Somercotes Power Station I was required to present my findings from the testing and evaluation of a new type of pump under consideration by management. Following my evaluation and subsequent presentation, management at the Power Station went ahead with the purchase.

High computer literacy

I am a keen computer user and regularly use the following packages:

- CAD
- MS Excel
- MS Word
- MS Project
- MS PowerPoint

Willingness to embrace new ideas

My thesis topic, 'Power: It's a passion', looked at applications of current technology to the generation of power in the future. The industry journal *Power Engineer* contacted me to write an article on the subject with the editorial suggesting that some of the ideas were 'at the forefront of thinking around the topic'. Besides undertaking university studies, to keep my knowledge up-to-date I regularly undertake my own research via the internet and numerous trade journals to determine industry trends and identify applications to my own work environment.

Education

2011–2014	Bachelor of Engineering (Electrical) Hons
	University of Chesterfield
	Honours Thesis: 'Power: It's a passion
2011	A Levels
	Beckenham Ladies' College
	Subjects: Mathematics; Physics; Politics

Academic achievements

2014	University Medal in Electrical Engineering
2014	Publication in *Power Engineer* entitled 'The Power or The Passion: Energy sources for the future'
2010	Rostrum Public Speaking Finalist
	Topic: 'Energy yesterday, today, tomorrow'

Employment history

July 2013–Sept 2013	Associate Electrical Engineer
	Summer Vacation Student, Somercotes Power Station, Alfreton

Responsibilities

- Assist electrical engineer in the design and layout of electrical installations and circuitry.
- Collect information, perform complex calculations and prepare diagrams and drawings of electrical installations and circuitry.
- Use CAD to produce designs and detailed drawings.
- Assist in testing and commissioning of electrical equipment and installations, and in the supervision of operations and maintenance.

Achievements
- New drawings for Somercotes Power Station No. 1 completed.
- Pump re-designed and installation programme outlined.

Interests and activities

University debating team, computer simulations, personal computing, cooking, hockey

Referees

Mr Eric Sykes	Prof. James Edwards
Manager, Somercotes Power Station	Head of School Electrical Engineering, UoC
01773 239777	01246 114678

An alternative makeover

The many engineering recruiters we have met prefer a more traditional layout with the emphasis on degree content (especially practical projects) and on relevant engineering experience. So with that in mind we present an alternative makeover for you to consider.

Josephine Brand

Address: 11 Ridgley St, Beckenham, Kent BR6 6AB
                     Telephone: (020) 8234 5678
Email address: J.Brand@techno.co.uk   Mobile: 07011 329897

Career objective

I am keen to build on my knowledge of electrical engineering gained from my degree and the analytical, communication and project management skills gained from my experience at Somercotes Power Station to develop a career within the power industry.

Education

2011–2014   BEng(Hons) Electrical Engineering
University of Chesterfield
Relevant modules included: Power Generation and Transmission, Power Electronics and Electromechanics, Project Management, Advanced Modern Management, Digital Control, Digital Systems Design
Final year research project, 'A feature comparison of pumped hydroelectric power storage systems', produced an online database allowing feature-by-feature comparison of components and system configurations for designing hydroelectric storage systems.

2011   A Levels
Beckenham Ladies' College
Subjects: Mathematics; Physics; Politics

Academic achievements

2014   University Medal in Electrical Engineering

2014   Publication in *Power Engineer* entitled 'The Power or The Passion: Energy sources for the future'

Employment history

July 2013–Sept 2013   Associate Electrical Engineer
Summer Vacation Student, Somercotes Power Station, Alfreton

Responsibilities

- Assist in testing and commissioning of electrical equipment and installations, and in the supervision of operations and maintenance.
- Assist electrical engineer in the design and layout of electrical installations and circuitry.
- Collect information, perform complex calculations and prepare diagrams and drawings of electrical installations and circuitry.
- Use CAD to produce designs and detailed drawings.

Achievements

- Pump re-designed and installation programme outlined.
- New drawings for Somercotes Power Station No. 1 completed.

Skills, experience and personal attributes

Speaking and presentation skills

I was a finalist at the National University debating challenge held in Oxford last year. While at Somercotes Power Station I was required to present my findings from the testing and evaluation of a new type of pump under consideration by management. Following my evaluation and subsequent presentation, management at the Power Station went ahead with the purchase.

High computer literacy

I regularly use the following packages and programming languages for university projects and my own personal projects:

- CAD: AutoCAD PCB and CIRCAD
- Simulation and modelling: Matlab and Simscape
- Ansys Finite Element Analysis
- Verilog
- C++ and Java
- Office software: Word, Excel, Access, PowerPoint, MS Project.

Willingness to embrace new ideas

Building on an assignment for my 'Power Generation and Transmission' module with independent research and interviews with industry specialists, I wrote an article, 'The Power or The Passion: Energy sources for the future. Applications of current technology to the generation of power in the future' which was accepted for publication in *Power Engineer* (Volume 24, p. 255). This involved having to research and address commercial, political and economic issues as well as practical engineering considerations.

Interests and activities

- Regular participant in the university debating team.
- Currently designing a mobile/tablet app to allow remote control of various electronic equipment in my house.

Referees

Mr Eric Sykes
Manager, Somercotes Power Station
01773 239777

Prof. James Edwards
Head of School Electrical Engineering, UoC
01246 114678

Graduate checklist

- Name, full address, telephone numbers, up-to-date email address (that reflects the image you want to portray)
- Full details of all paid jobs you have held
- Details of any voluntary work you may have done
- Full educational qualifications including details of any modules and projects relevant to the role
- Details of any relevant or interesting extra-curricular activities
- Emphasis on achievements and results
- Believable competency statements backed up with evidence
- A snappy career statement
- Printed on high-quality paper or emailed in PDF format
- Two referees (whom you have already approached), including full contact details.

Early career

The early career job hunter will be looking to gain further experience and promotion. They will be trying to maximise their limited experience and develop the necessary skills for the next step, or a broader portfolio of skills to make themselves more employable. The challenges here are to demonstrate that you are a more experienced candidate than graduate applicants. You need to make your recent job experience count so potential employers can see that you will 'hit the ground running' in the new position and that you will not need a lot of hand holding and basic training. Employers need to understand not just what you have previously done, but what you are capable of in the future.

Training Manager
Handle Sisters Pharmaceuticals

Would you like to join the world's third biggest pharmaceutical company, currently expanding rapidly in the European market? We require a manager to join our training division, where you would be responsible for the delivery of training programmes to our sales staff.

A motivated, results-focused team player, you will have excellent communication skills, and will be able to handle pressure and work to deadlines. With several years of solid experience in a multinational, you will be accredited in NLP and will have a basic understanding of training evaluation techniques. Reporting to our Regional Manager, you will be required to provide input into the marketing strategies for the European region by training our sales staff to improve market share.

Handle Sisters are Equal Opportunity employers.

Please forward your CV to: Linda Spark, Personnel Dept, Handle Sisters Pharmaceuticals, 58 Boundary Street, London EC1 2LP.

The 'before' CV

Personal Details of Ms Jenny Saunders:

- 15 Browns Rd
- Alfreton
- DE55 9ZZ
- Telephone: (01773) 588888
- Fax number: (01773) 588889
- Email: Jenny@comten.net

> This candidate will go to the bottom of the shortlist with a bullet. Overuse of bullets leads to a long and messy document that looks a bit like a computer program print-out – use bullet points judiciously

> Poorly worded and repetitive career objective statement that is not especially compelling

Career objective

- I am keen to build a career with a progressive learning organisation that genuinely values the contribution that training can make to achieving business objectives.

Skills, experience and personal attributes

- Business acumen

  - In my current role at Fish Fingers Inc. I am required to analyse business reports (e.g. sales, production) and identify training opportunities.
  - By reviewing sales figures and talking to representatives I discovered that many were having trouble overcoming sales rejections.
  - Training was designed to address this problem and sales increased by 25% two months after training.
  - My practical experience is supplemented by graduate management qualifications from the University of Scunthorpe.

- Knowledge of training techniques

  - In addition to completing qualifications in adult education, I am an accredited NLP trainer (Level IV) and have conducted evaluations on all training courses conducted to date.
  - As a member of the Institute of Training and Development, I undertake professional development so that I am continually updating my knowledge.
  - In this way, I ensure that I maximise use of the best available training techniques.

- **<u>Ability to motivate others</u>**

  These are more a list of activities than achievements

  - Convince sales representatives to attend out-of-hours training
  - Present job-related and relevant courses
  - Conduct a training needs analysis
  - Conduct evaluations of training courses

<u>Education</u>

- 2008 – 2011 BA (Adult Education)
  - University of Scunthorpe
- Graduate Management Qualification

  Looks like an additional postgraduate qualification here that will slip between the cracks

  - London Graduate School of Management
- <u>Short courses</u>
  - NLP (Level IV) accreditation
    - Training for Success
  - New techniques in course evaluation
    - Institute of Training and Development
  - Games Trainers Play
    - Training Mind-Gym Inc.

<u>Academic achievements</u>

- Best Trainer (as evaluated by practicum trainees)
- Awarded by the ITD

<u>Employment history</u>

- Feb 2014 – current Assistant Training Manager, Fish Fingers Inc., Riddings, Derbyshire

<u>Responsibilities</u>

- identify training needs based on business objectives
- prepare business training plan
- design NLP-based training courses

- conduct training courses
- evaluate and report on learning outcomes
- manage training budget and expenditure
- manage department of three staff.

It just goes on and on and the most important section on achievements is almost lost at the end

Achievements

- 80% of courses conducted out of core business hours to minimise selling downtime
- in-house designed sales training course contributed to 25% increase in sales
- participant and manager satisfaction ratings of 4 and above for 85% of courses
- training budget on target (£150,000) and expenditure on external consultants reduced by 18%.

- Jan 2012 – Jan 2014 Training Officer, Bakers Dozen, Ryde, Hampshire

Referees

Mr Winston Place
Managing Director, Fish Inc.
(01773) 123456

Dr Tom Baker
Training Manager
(01773) 123467

A great set of results that is shot down in flames by a hail of bullets

The 'after' CV

Jenny Saunders

Address: 15 Browns Rd
Alfreton
DE55 9ZZ

Telephone: (01773) 588888
Fax: (01773) 588889
Email: JennyS@comten.net

Career objective

I want to contribute to a progressive learning organisation that genuinely values the contribution that training makes to achieving business objectives.

Skills, experience and personal attributes

Business acumen

In my current role at Fish Fingers Inc. I am required to analyse business reports (e.g. sales, production) and identify training opportunities. By reviewing sales figures and talking to representatives I discovered that many were having trouble overcoming sales rejections. Training was designed to address this problem and sales increased by 25% two months after training. My practical experience is supplemented by graduate management qualifications from the University of Scunthorpe.

Knowledge of training techniques

In addition to completing qualifications in adult education, I am an accredited NLP trainer (Level IV) and have conducted evaluations on all training courses conducted to date. As a member of the Institute of Training and Development, I undertake professional development so that I am continually updating my knowledge. In this way, I ensure that I maximise use of the best available training techniques.

Ability to motivate others

At FF Inc. training courses often need to be run after hours or on weekends, cutting into sales representatives' personal lives. It is important from participants' perspectives that the courses are considered worthwhile, help them to deliver results on-the-job and are fun. To ensure that the trainees' needs were met, on appointment at FF Inc. I interviewed a cross-section of representatives, identified their greatest needs and designed training courses to address these. Evaluations have proven these to be very successful, with participant and manager satisfaction ratings of 4 and above for 85% of courses.

Education

Tertiary

2008 – 2011	**BA (Adult Education)** University of Scunthorpe
2012 – 2014	**Graduate Management Qualification** London Graduate School of Management

Short courses

2012	**NLP (Level IV) accreditation** Training for Success
2013	**New techniques in course evaluation** Institute of Training and Development
2014	**Games Trainers Play** Training Mind-Gym Inc.

Academic achievements

2007	**Best Trainee in Adult Education (as evaluated by practicum trainees)** Awarded by the ITD

Employment history

Assistant Training Manager   Fish Fingers Inc, Riddings, Derbyshire
Feb 2014 – current

Responsibilities

Identify training needs based on business objectives, prepare business training plan, design NLP-based training courses, conduct training courses, evaluate and report on learning outcomes, manage training budget and expenditure, manage department of three staff.

Achievements

- 80% of courses conducted out of core business hours to minimise selling downtime

- in-house designed sales training course contributed to 25% increase in sales

- participant and manager satisfaction ratings of 4 and above for 85% of courses

- training budget on target (£150,000) and expenditure on external consultants reduced by 18%.

Training Officer   Bakers Dozen, Ryde, Hampshire
                            Jan 2012 – Jan 2014

Responsibilities

Evaluate off-the-shelf training courses and other training resources (e.g. videos), conduct off-the-shelf training courses, prepare training materials, report on training activity, gather information on training needs, evaluate in-house courses, maintain training records.

Achievements

- implemented structured induction training courses for all new starters

- conducted courses according to training manager's training plan (on time and on budget)

- implemented new computerised training record keeping system.

Team Member   McDonald's, Portsmouth
                            Jan 2008 – Dec 2011

Referees

Mr Winston Place   Dr Tom Baker
Managing Director, Fish Inc.   Time Manager
(01773) 123456   (01773) 123467

An alternative makeover

Recruiters might ask why Jenny's most relevant experience was relegated to the last page of her CV. As she has very relevant experience and because the advertisement specifically asks for 'solid experience' we might encourage this person to consider putting their work experience first and to incorporate their competency statements into the description of their experience – where most of the evidence comes from anyway. We have redesigned the CV along these lines below to illustrate how you can move elements of the CV around to increase the fit with the advertisement.

Jenny Saunders

Address: 15 Browns Rd, Alfreton
Telephone: (01773) 588888 – Email: JennyS@comten.net

Career objective

I want to contribute to a progressive learning organisation that genuinely values the contribution training makes to achieving business objectives.

Relevant experience

Feb 2014 – current   Assistant Training Manager, Fish Fingers Inc,
Riddings, Derbyshire

Key responsibilities

Identifying training needs based on business objectives, preparing business training plan, designing and delivering NLP-based training courses, evaluating and measuring learning outcomes, managing training budget of £150,000, managing a department of three staff.

Relevant skills, attributes and achievements

Results focus: By reviewing sales figures and talking to representatives I discovered that many were having trouble overcoming sales rejections. I designed training to address this problem and sales increased by 25% two months after training. Conducted a review of the training programme which led to shifting 80% of courses out of core business hours to minimise selling downtime and an 18% reduction in spending on external trainers.

Training programme delivery: Delivered a range of NLP-based training to sales representatives and managers, using face-to-face workshops, online learning and remote teaching via webinars. Achieved a satisfaction rating of 'very good' or 'excellent' for 85% of courses.

Communication and ability to motivate: Conducted interviews with sales representatives and managers to assess their needs and frustrations with existing training. I redesigned the training programme making it more relevant and more fun and broke the training down into smaller chunks to make it more flexible. Because of this I was able to persuade participants to take part in training outside their core hours, even to the extent of giving up their personal time.

Jan 2012 – Jan 2014 Training Officer Baker's Dozen, Ryde, Hampshire

Key responsibilities

Evaluated off-the-shelf training courses and other training resources (e.g. videos), delivered training courses, prepared materials, drafted reports on training activities, gathered information on training needs, evaluated in-house courses, maintained accurate training records.

Achievements

- implemented structured induction training courses for all new starters
- conducted courses according to training manager's training plan (on time and on budget)
- implemented new computerised training record keeping system.

Other skills

Knowledge of training techniques

In addition to completing qualifications in adult education, I am an accredited NLP trainer (Level IV) and have conducted evaluations on all training courses conducted to date. As a member of the Institute of Training and Development, I undertake professional development so that I am continually updating my knowledge. In this way, I ensure that I maximise use of the best available training techniques.

Education

2008–2011	BA (Adult Education), University of Scunthorpe
2012–2014	Graduate Management Qualification, London Graduate School of Management

Short courses

2012	NLP (Level IV) accreditation, Training for Success
2013	New techniques in course evaluation, Institute of Training and Development
2014	Games Trainers Play, Training Mind-Gym Inc.

Academic achievements

2007	Best Trainee in Adult Education (as evaluated by practicum trainees), awarded by the ITD

Other experience

Team Member	McDonald's, Portsmouth Jan 2008–Dec 2011

Referees

Mr Winston Place	Dr Tom Baker
Managing Director,	Fish Inc. Time Manager
(01773) 123456	(01773) 123467

Early career checklist

- Name, full address, telephone numbers, up-to-date email address
- Full details of all your experience relevant to the job
- Details of any voluntary work you may have done that has developed relevant skills
- Full educational qualifications and relevant training including relevant short courses post graduation
- Emphasis on achievements and results, not just responsibilities
- Believable competency statements backed up with evidence

- Answer the 'what's in it for me' question for the employer
- Evidence that you have moved beyond graduate-level capability
- Snappy career statement
- Printed on high-quality paper or emailed as PDF
- Two referees (whom you have already approached), including full contact details

Mid-career

The mid-career candidate is likely to have developed a broad portfolio of skills as well as showing some specialisation and achievement in at least one of those areas. The mid-career applicant is more likely to have a history of managing teams or groups or, failing that, a sustained history of achievement within their specialisation. The mid-career person who is ambitious will be looking for a position that will provide a springboard to the higher echelons of their profession. Alternatively, mid-career applicants may be looking to consolidate their position and broaden their experience by moving from one industry sector (such as Banking and Finance) to another (such as Manufacturing). Finally, mid-career applicants may be embarking on a change of career direction. Depending on how radical the change is, the mid-career change applicant might apply for positions at the equivalent level in the new career, or they may decide to start at a relatively lower place on the new career ladder in order to get a look in.

The challenge for the mid-career applicant is to present their experience as a strong selling point, and to try to convey continued enthusiasm and passion for what it is they are doing. Recruiters will be on the look out for signs of burnout or disillusionment (perhaps evidenced by a rapid succession of brief appointments over the past couple of years). If you have held any positions for less than a year, be prepared to provide an explanation for this that paints you in a positive light.

FINANCIAL ACCOUNTANT

This is a fixed-term contract for a modern manufacturing site.

Although supervising five people, the position is very much 'hands on', which requires a willingness to take on detail and the ability to juggle multiple tasks.

We seek a computer-literate accountant, with experience of Microsoft systems and accounting experience, which must include tax and general ledger. You will need to be a CPA or ACA and possess strong written and verbal communication skills; ideally you will have manufacturing experience. However, it is unlikely that candidates with less than five years' accounting experience will have sufficient background for the position.

This opportunity is available now.

Please call or send details to Mark Matthews,
Person Ltd, South St, Edinburgh EH4 3TL
Tel: (0131) 746 7132
Fax: (0131) 746 7123

The 'before' CV

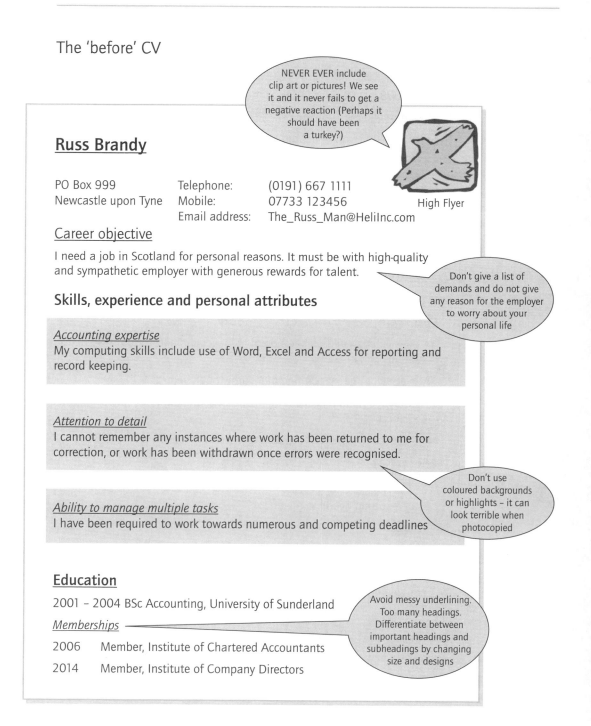

Russ Brandy

PO Box 999
Newcastle upon Tyne

Telephone: (0191) 667 1111
Mobile: 07733 123456
Email address: The_Russ_Man@HeliInc.com

High Flyer

NEVER EVER include clip art or pictures! We see it and it never fails to get a negative reaction (Perhaps it should have been a turkey?)

Career objective

I need a job in Scotland for personal reasons. It must be with high-quality and sympathetic employer with generous rewards for talent.

Don't give a list of demands and do not give any reason for the employer to worry about your personal life

Skills, experience and personal attributes

Accounting expertise
My computing skills include use of Word, Excel and Access for reporting and record keeping.

Attention to detail
I cannot remember any instances where work has been returned to me for correction, or work has been withdrawn once errors were recognised.

Don't use coloured backgrounds or highlights – it can look terrible when photocopied

Ability to manage multiple tasks
I have been required to work towards numerous and competing deadlines

Education

2001 – 2004 BSc Accounting, University of Sunderland

Memberships

2006   Member, Institute of Chartered Accountants

2014   Member, Institute of Company Directors

Avoid messy underlining. Too many headings. Differentiate between important headings and subheadings by changing size and designs

Employment history

Dec 2009 – current Financial Controller, Helicopters Inc., Middlesbrough

Responsibilities

- preparation, consolidation and review of management and project reporting
- overseeing the preparation of progress claims and analysis and reporting on cashflow
- controlling and covering all foreign exchange exposures
- ensuring that all insurance requirements for the project and contract are met
- liaison with banks for provision of security required under the contracts and subcontracts
- supervision of two accounting staff.

Feb 2005 – Nov 2009 Assistant Financial Controller, Helicopters Inc.

Responsibilities

- consolidation and preparation of management and statutory accounts, tax returns and budgets
- overseeing the preparation of monthly board reports
- developing and implementing foreign exchange trading procedures and systems
- review and support of capital expenditure proposals.

Achievements

- implemented new foreign exchange trading procedures and systems
- all reporting deadlines met.

Referees

Mr Fred Scuttle,   Mr Robert Todd

Managing Director, Helicopters Inc.   Chairman, Helicopters Inc.

(01642) 991230 (01642) 991234

Looks like he is very busy achieving absolutely nothing.

Watch out for disasters with formatting – for some reason using tabs to space material can lead to all sorts of nastiness when printed out on someone else's computer. Always check the final product

Poor layout, few achievements, no attempt to address the selection criteria, career objective counter-productive and reads as a set of demands and also hints at personal turmoil – not a good look!

The 'after' CV

This CV makeover outlines Benjamin's competences in a more persuasive way. We have removed the clip art and desperation from his CV. The layout looks more professional and it is easier to read.

Russell Brandy

42 River View Drive   Telephone: (0191) 667 1111
Newcastle upon Tyne   Mobile: (07733) 123456
Email address: RussellB@HeliInc.com

Career objective

To secure a busy 'hands-on' senior financial role that provides challenge and capitalises on my accounting expertise. I am keen to find a position closer to home so that I can combine professional with personal fulfilment.

Skills, experience and personal attributes

Accounting expertise

Having a varied finance background in both the public and private sector, I feel confident in my ability to fulfil the role of financial accountant as outlined. My experience in the taxation office has provided me with a thorough understanding of financial reporting requirements. Whilst at Helicopters Inc. I have worked primarily in taxation and general ledger. I am familiar with a range of accounting software packages such as Sage and Agresso, and have designed in-house accounting tools using Microsoft Excel integrated with a product database in Access.

Attention to detail

Attention to detail is an essential performance criteria in my current role at Helicopters Inc., and I have always been rated as 'Highly Commendable' in this area. I pride myself on delivering a quality reporting product that the management team can have confidence in. I cannot remember any instances where work has been returned to me for correction, or work has been withdrawn once errors were recognised.

Ability to manage multiple tasks

On a number of occasions I have had to manage the end of year reporting whilst implementing new accounting systems and training new members of my team. Despite these challenges, I have always successfully fulfilled my demanding deadlines through careful planning and effective delegation.

Employment history

Financial Controller   Helicopters Inc., Middlesbrough

Dec 2009 – current

Responsibilities

Preparation, consolidation and review of management and project reporting, overseeing the preparation of progress claims and analysis and reporting on cashflow, controlling and covering all foreign exchange exposures, ensuring that all insurance requirements for the project and contract are met, liaison with banks for provision of security required under the contracts and sub-contracts, supervision of two accounting staff.

Achievements

- Implemented new project reporting system to suit management team needs
- Met all management reporting deadlines
- Reduced time spent on compiling information in department by 65%
- Substituted for company secretary in his absence.

Assistant Financial Controller   Helicopters Inc., Middlesbrough

Feb 2005 – Nov 2009

Responsibilities

Consolidation and preparation of management and statutory accounts, tax returns and budgets, review and analysis of operating results for senior management, overseeing the preparation for monthly board reports, developing and implementing foreign exchange trading procedures and systems, review and support of capital expenditure proposals.

Achievements

- Implemented new foreign exchange trading procedures and systems
- All reporting deadlines met.

Education

2001 – 2004   BSc Accounting University of Sunderland

Memberships

2006   Member, Institute of Chartered Accountants
2014   Member, Institute of Company Directors

Referees

Mr Fred Scuttle,   Mr Robert Todd
Managing Director, Helicopters Inc.   Chairman, Helicopters Inc.
(01642) 991230   (01642) 991234

Mid-career checklist

- Name, full address, telephone numbers, up-to-date email address
- Full details of all paid jobs you have held
- Details of any voluntary work you may have undertaken
- Full educational qualifications
- Emphasis on achievements and results
- Believable competency statements backed up with evidence
- Evidence of sustained achievement
- Evidence of energy and enthusiasm
- Snappy career statement if changing career
- Printed on high-quality paper
- Two referees (whom you have already approached), including full contact details

Mature career

Candidates with a mature career are likely to have been working for perhaps 15 to 20 years, which conventionally would put them in their forties or above. Recruiters will be looking for applicants in this pool who have demonstrated successful and extensive management skills, perhaps across a range of industry sectors. Often roles at this level will be focused on developing plans and strategies for the business, and it is often the case that the technical skills that got you to this point are going to be less important than managerial skills, reputation and potential managerial skills. The challenge for some will be to demonstrate they are now ready for the move up from a technical focus to a broader 'bigger picture' focus, and also that they possess good commercial and/or political skills. This is not the place for the tactless blunderer or people who cannot read a profit and loss account!

GENERAL MANAGER – TECHNOLOGY

Our client, a leading national retailer, is seeking a General Manager to lead their business in a period of strong growth here in the UK and overseas.

The role

Principally the role will focus on developing a strategic IT plan that supports business objectives and future system requirements. There is a need to review and evaluate existing hardware/software and to manage a small support team.

The person

You are a business manager first and foremost who understands the retail industry. You have a thorough understanding of information technology, including current and future directions across the internet/intranet and extranet. You possess strong people management skills and appreciate the importance of getting the best out of your staff. You have exceptional presentation skills and can tailor content to suit a broad audience. Excellent written presentation skills are required to communicate organisational needs and persuade senior management to implement system changes. This is an excellent opportunity for a successful individual to join a rapidly developing organisation and make an impact on its future direction.

Send CV to:
Claudia Joy
Claudia Joy Ltd
PO Box 7
London WC1E 2PL

The 'before' CV

CV

Chrissy O'Dowd
432 Heaven Road
Swansea
Telephone: (01792) 123456
Mobile: 07776 876543
Email:Try@turningitoff.com

The Courier font is looking dated and makes it look as though a typewriter was used

Skills, experience and personal attributes

As the group leader in Information Technology I am required to identify the strategic technological and systems requirements of all retail stores.

Leadership

Avoid this commonly recommended two-column layout – it wastes page real estate, puts too much emphasis on the heading or dates and leaves not enough space to set out your achievements neatly

This is achieved by linking current and anticipated business needs with available technology. The Internet shopping site is a prime example of this. Leading a team of store managers, merchandising managers and IT managers we identified business needs,concerns and strategies. Under my leadership the site was developed and launched within 18 months of conception.

Knowledge of the retail industry

I have worked in the retail industry for all of my working life, starting out at the bottom as a retail assistant, moving into a role as Customer Service Manager, leading an in-store IT team as the IT Manager and finally working my way up to a state-based corporate role. My unique grounding enables me to fully understand the day-to-day operations of a store as well as its management.

Business management

In my role as Senior Manager, New Technology, I am required to demonstrate a sound knowledge of each store's business requirements and strategic direction. I have supplemented my work experience with formal studies in a Masters of Business Administration. Key projects that I have been involved with that have resulted in both cost savings and efficiency improvements include: implementing a fully integrated communication system and selecting a supplier resulting in an average cost saving of £500,000 per store; introducing new technology to better monitor in-store trading patterns and provide links back to staffing requirements; implementing new POS technology without disruption to trading pattern

Education

2010 – 2012	Masters of Business Administration University of Edinburgh
2003 – 2005	BSc Information Technology University of Technology, London
2005 – 2006	Certificate IV — retail strategic management, East Croydon College

Employment history

Dec 2008 – current	Senior Manager, New Technology, Raspberry Holdings Ltd, Head Office (Swansea)

Duties included:

- indirect responsibility for all instore IT Managers
- development of corporate IT plan
- management of corporate IT objectives
- monitoring of IT standards across stores
- identification and selection of hardware and software for stores' in-house use
- implementation of new online shopping systems; implementation of intranet and video technology linking stores integration and

selection of other new
technology including POS,
telephones, paging
- management team on-floor
communication.

Achievements:
- fully integrated communication
system and supplier introduced
to all stores over an 18-month
period with an average cost
saving of £500,000 per store
- all IT objectives outlined
incorporate plan achieved
- introduction of weekly video
conferencing with IT in-store
managers to ensure sharing of
best practice and improve
communication
- online shopping system
introduced returning £10 million
in first week of operation with
average growth of 15% per week
and no loss of sales to
individual stores.

Dec 2005 – Nov 2008 IT Manager, Raspberry Holdings
Ltd, Newport

Duties included:
- management of IT team (3 staff)
- maintenance of in-store systems
evaluation of software for store
- testing of new software for
store
- implementation of new software
- implementation of back-up and
recovery systems.

It's starting to look like a list and it just keeps going on and on and on and...

Achievements:
- identified and introduced new
technology 'Sales to Staffing'
to better monitor in-store
trading patterns and provide
links back to staffing
requirements
- implementation of new POS
technology without disruption
to trading pattern

- recovery systems worked in 100% of all cases, resulting in no down time due to computer failure
- recruited and developed own replacement over a two-year period.

Dec 2000 – Nov 2005 Customer Service Manager, Raspberry Holdings Ltd, Newport

Duties included:
- staff scheduling
- performance management
- training and development
- monitoring service standards
- stock management and merchandising
- management of budgets for 'Homewares'
- management and staff utilisation reporting
- organising special product promotions.

The format makes the CV look overly long and repetitious. It gives the impression that the candidate does not really know his way around document-creation software. Perhaps he even has a secretary?

Achievements:
- budgets on target 85% of the time
- sales targets achieved and exceeded by 85%
- named 'Customer Service Manager' of the year by the store manager
- successful selection and promotion of two staff members to the customer service manager traineeship.

Summary of other jobs Dec 1998– Nov 2000 Raspberry Holdings Ltd, Newport

Referees   Mr Harold Seccombe, Raspberry Holdings Ltd, Swansea
                   Mr Stephen Milligan
                   Ying Tong IT Ltd, Didlipoh St, Newport

Not a bad CV from a content point of view, but let down badly with this out-of-date and difficult-to-read layout. This layout is probably the most common we see but that is not a recommendation!

The 'after' CV

Christian O'Dowd

432 Heaven Road

Swansea

Email: chauncy@gardener.com

Telephone: (01792) 123456

Mobile: (07776) 876543

Career objective

To contribute to the successful growth and management of a retailing organisation by leading initiatives to link business needs with technological solutions.

Skills, experience and personal attributes

Leadership

As the group leader in Information Technology I am required to identify the strategic technological and systems requirements of all retail stores. This is achieved by linking current and anticipated business needs with available technology. The Internet shopping site is a prime example of this. Leading a team of store managers, merchandising managers and IT managers we identified business needs, concerns and strategies. Under my leadership the site was developed and launched within 18 months of conception.

Knowledge of the retail industry

I have worked in the retail industry for all of my working life, starting out at the bottom as a retail assistant, moving into a role as Customer Service Manager, leading an in-store IT team as the IT Manager and finally working my way up to a state-based corporate role. My unique grounding enables me to fully understand the day-to-day operations of a store as well as its management.

Business management

In my role as Senior Manager, New Technology, I am required to demonstrate a sound knowledge of each store's business requirements and strategic direction. I have supplemented my work experience with formal studies in a Masters of Business Administration. Key projects that I have been involved with that have resulted in both cost savings and efficiency improvements include: fully integrated communication system and supplier resulting in an average cost saving of £500,000 per store; introduction of new technology to better monitor in-store trading patterns and provide links back to staffing requirements; implemented new POS technology without disruption to trading pattern.

Employment history

Senior Manager New Technology Raspberry Holdings Ltd, Head Office (Swansea)
Dec 2008 – current
Duties included
Indirect responsibility for all in-store IT managers, development of corporate IT plan, management of corporate IT objectives, monitoring of IT standards across stores, identification and selection of hardware and software for stores' in-house use, implementation of new online shopping systems, implementation of intranet and video technology linking stores, integration and selection of other new technology including POS, telephones, paging, management team on-floor communication.

Achievements

- Fully integrated communication system and supplier introduced to all stores over an 18-month period with an average cost saving of £500,000 per store
- All IT objectives outlined in corporate plan achieved
- Introduction of weekly video conferencing with IT in-store managers to ensure sharing of best practice and improve communication
- Online shopping system introduced returning £10 million in first week of operation with average growth of 15% per week and no loss of sales to individual stores.

IT Manager   Raspberry Holdings Ltd, Newport
Dec 2005 – Nov 2008
Duties included
Management of IT team (three staff), maintenance of in-store systems, evaluation of software for store, testing of new software for store, implementation of new software, implementation of back-up and recovery systems.

Achievements

- Identified and introduced new technology 'Sales to Staffing' to better monitor in-store trading patterns and provide links back to staffing requirements
- Implementation of new POS technology without disruption to trading pattern
- Recovery systems worked in 100% of all cases, resulting in no down time due to computer failure
- Recruited and developed own replacement over a two-year period.

Customer Service Manager   Raspberry Holdings Ltd, Newport
                                  Dec 2000 – Nov 2005

Duties included

Management of retail service team including staff scheduling, performance management, training and development, monitoring service standards, stock management and merchandising, management of budgets for 'Homewares', management and staff utilisation reporting, organising special product promotions.

Achievements

- Budgets on target 85% of the time
- Sales targets achieved and exceeded plan by 85%
- Named 'Customer Service Manager' of the year by the store manager
- Successful selection and promotion of two staff members to the customer service manager traineeship.

Summary of other jobs

Dec 1998 – Nov 2000   Raspberry Holdings Ltd, Retail Assistant Newport

Education

Masters of Business Administration University of Edinburgh 2010 – 2012
BSc of Information Technology University of Technology, London 2003 – 2005
Certificate IV – retail strategic management East Croydon College 2001 – 2002

Referees

Mr Harold Seccombe   Mr Stephen Milligan
Raspberry Holdings Ltd   Ying Tong IT Ltd
Swansea   Didlipoh St
01792 909909   Newport 01633 665363

Mature career checklist

- Name, full address, telephone numbers, up-to-date email address
- Details of all relevant jobs you have held, omitting trivial or very low-level positions from early career

- Details of any voluntary work you may have done if it demonstrates leadership or responsible community involvement commensurate with your executive status
- Full educational qualifications
- Emphasis on achievements and results
- Believable competency statements backed up with evidence
- Evidence of sustained achievement
- Evidence of energy and enthusiasm
- Evidence of people management and size of team
- Evidence of abilities to step up or across into strategic management if relevant to the position
- Printed on high-quality paper
- Two referees (whom you have already approached), including full contact details.

Returning from a break

Many people have a break in their career for all sorts of reasons. Some of these reasons are:

- having a baby
- caring for a family member
- injury or illness
- travel
- relocation of a partner
- redundancy or unemployment
- further training or education.

Despite what some commentators say, our research found that employers did not look favourably on breaks in employment unless it was for full-time academic study. However, you can easily make up for this by working hard to target your CV to the job advertisement. Gaps should be explained briefly, and you should quickly move on to paint a positive picture of where you see yourself going and how you can contribute to the company.

Don't be tempted to dwell on negative events such as an illness. Instead, the message to get across is that the period when the gap occurred is now completely behind you and that you are ready and willing to go once more and have a significant contribution to make to this organisation!

COMPUTER ANALYST/PROGRAMMER

An outstanding opportunity exists to join our leading edge Software Consultancy as an Analyst Programmer using the latest client/server technology. We are looking for creative and innovative thinkers who have a strong desire to be the best they can be in an environment that promotes vast opportunities and rewards to dedicated and determined staff. You will be working and/or be trained alongside some of the best software developers in the field. Experience in Visual Basic, Access, SQL Server, and Internet development with tertiary qualifications would be highly regarded. If you are ambitious and have an enthusiastic personality, you are ideal for these challenging and exciting roles.

Top salary and remuneration, bonuses and incentives, with available national and/or international travel opportunities on offer to the right applicant/s.

Send CV to:

Human Resources Director
Softly Softly Ltd
Lock Hill St
Sheffield, S. Yorks
S21 9PT

The 'before' CV

Miranda Hart

15 Fox Trot Avenue, Dudley, West Midlands

Telephone: (01384) 034510

Email: Miranda@home.co.uk

Married

1 child: Demi-Tess, born May 2012.

Irrelevant and possibly off-putting personal detail – omit

Another appallingly self-centred career objective – avoid jokes, sarcasm and personal detail

Career objective

To get back some sanity and adult company after the birth of my daughter Demi-Tess Hart and subsequent career break. To use the skills I learnt through the hard slog at uni to retrain. To get my previously successful career back on track.

Ability to develop new products

Focus on how you can replicate your success, not how long ago it was

Some time ago I wrote two award-winning and innovative software packages ('Ms Terry Investigates' and 'Y? Y? Y?') with sales of the latter package exceeding budget expectations by 150% (£2.3 million). During my university course I wrote two additional products judged by Human Side Ltd to be the best software products available of their kind. My course has provided me with up-to-date knowledge in Visual Basic, Access, SQL Server, and Internet technology.

Ambitious

With several years' experience in programming and product development I am now keen to fulfil my ultimate potential in a demanding and challenging role at Softly, Softly Ltd. While at Educational Software I was promoted from the role of programmer to senior programmer within two years based on my performance. When I relocated with my partner to Dudley, I took the opportunity to pursue relevant studies, so that up-to-date knowledge would help me to achieve my future career goals.

This makes the employer think, 'Will she pack up and leave again?' Just focus on developing knowledge that contributes to career goals

Knowledge of client/server technology

I led a project team exploring the application of client/server technology to a large telecommunications company. Using C/ST we were able to help the client to introduce a complex customer billing system that was simple and more cost-effective; am familiar with many of the client/servers and their capabilities through my own Internet research.

Education

2003 – 2009	BSc Information Technology
	University of Lowestoft
1998 – 1999	Certificate in Information Technology
	Great Yarmouth FE College
1997	A levels, Great Yarmouth High School
	Subjects: Mathematics, English, History,
	Geography, Business Studies

Academic achievements

2009	Best university software product
	Awarded by Human Side Ltd
2010	Best university educational software product
	Awarded by Human Side Ltd

Employment history

Feb 1999 – Mar 2012 Senior Programmer, Educational Software, Norwich

Responsibilities

- as for 'Programmer' (see below) with additional responsibility for the supervision, development and performance management of eight software programmers

Achievements

- team responsible for seven award-winning packages during the period I was supervising
- sales of educational packages increased by 80% during the period I was supervising.

Feb 1999 – Jan 2001 Programmer, Educational Software, Norwich

Responsibilities

- document computer user's requirements with analysts
- analyse objectives and software requirements identified by analysts
- write programs for educational software
- prepare support documentation for computer users and support personnel
- test and evaluate programs prepared by other programmers.

Achievements

- wrote 'Ms Terry Investigates', winner of the 1999 educational software package of the year
- sales of educational package 'Y? Y? Y?' exceeded budget expectations by 150% (£2.3 million).

Jan 1997 – Jan 1999 PC Support Officer, Legal Eagles, Lowestoft

Responsibilities

- software and hardware selection
- testing software prior to installation
- systems planning
- installation of software and hardware systems
- maintenance of systems
- basic programming

With this type of formatting it is easy to get lost in the detail

Achievements

- installation of major software upgrade (150 users) without loss of business trading time
- selection of software package that saved £50K in business operating expenses.

Interests and activities

New Internet products, interactive computer games.

Referees

Mr Rhufus T. Firefly	Mr Sydney Rumpo
General Manager	Office Manager
Educational Software	Legal Eagles
1 Racecourse Drive	12 Possit St
Norwich	Lowestoft

The 'after' CV

Miranda Hart

15 Fox Trot Avenue
Dudley, West Midlands

Telephone: (01384) 034510
Email: M. Hart@work.co.uk

Career objective

To utilise my analytical and creative programming experience in developing innovative products within a commercial consultancy environment.

Skills, experience and personal attributes

Ability to develop new products

I have previously written award-winning and innovative software packages ('Ms Terry Investigates' and 'Y? Y? Y?') with sales of the latter package exceeding budget expectations by 150% (£2.3 million). During my university course I wrote two additional products judged by Human Side Ltd to be the best software products available of their kind. My course has provided me with up-to-date knowledge in Visual Basic, Access, SQL Server and Internet technology.

Ambitions

While at Educational Software I was promoted from the role of programmer to senior programmer within two years based on my performance. When I relocated with my partner to Dudley, I took the opportunity to pursue relevant studies, so that up-to-date knowledge would help me to achieve my future career goals.

Knowledge of client/server technology

I led a project team exploring the application of client/server technology to a large telecommunications company. Using C/ST we were able to help the client to introduce a complex customer billing system that was simple and more cost effective. I am familiar with many of the client/servers and their capabilities through my own self-directed reading.

Education

2003 – 2009	BSc Information Technology University of Lowestoft
1998 – 1999	Certificate in Information Technology Great Yarmouth FE College
1997	A levels, Great Yarmouth High School Subjects: Mathematics, English, History, Geography, Business Studies

Academic achievements

2009	Best university software product Awarded by Human Side Ltd
2008	Best university educational software product Awarded by Human Side Ltd

Employment history

Senior Programmer   Educational Software, Norwich
Feb 2001 – Mar 2012

Responsibilities

As for 'Programmer' (see below) with additional responsibility for the supervision, development and performance management of eight software programmers.

Achievements

- Team responsible for seven award-winning packages during the period I was supervising
- Sales of educational packages increased by 80% during the period I was supervising.

Programmer

Feb 1999 – Jan 2001   Educational Software, Norwich

Responsibilities

Document computer user's requirements with analysts, analyse objectives and software requirements identified by analysts, write programs for educational software, prepare support documentation for computer users and support personnel, test and evaluate programs prepared by other programmers.

Achievements

- Wrote 'Ms Terry Investigates', winner of the 1999 educational software package of the year
- Sales of educational package 'Y? Y? Y?' exceeded budget expectations by 150% (£2.3 million).

PC support Officer   Legal Eagles, Lowestoft

Jan 1997 – Jan 1999

Responsibilities

Software and hardware selection, testing software prior to installation, systems planning, installation of software and hardware systems, maintenance of systems, basic programming.

Achievements

- Installation of major software upgrade (150 users) without loss of business trading time
- Selection of software package that saved £50,000 in business operating expenses.

Interests and activities

New Internet products, interactive computer games.

Referees

Mr Rhufus T. Firefly
General Manager
Educational Software
1 Racecourse Drive
Norwich

Mr Sydney Rumpo
Office Manager
Legal Eagles
12 Possit St
Lowestoft

Returning from a break checklist

- Name, full address, telephone numbers, up-to-date email address
- Full details of all paid jobs you have held
- Details of any voluntary work you may have done
- Full educational qualifications
- Emphasis on achievements and results
- Emphasize up-to-date skill set and current knowledge
- Believable competency statements backed with evidence
- Not dwelling on the gaps
- Evidence of energy and enthusiasm
- Snappy career statement focusing on future contributions you can make
- Printed on high-quality paper
- Two referees (whom you have already approached), including full contact details

Career change

Two of the buzz-phrases in the human resources area are 'transferable skills' and 'transfer of training'. All they mean is taking something you learned in one place and using it successfully in another. If you have ever played golf, you might have practised for hours on the driving range to perfect your swing, but the real test comes when you are out on the course in a match tournament. Some groups of people have skills that overlap a lot, so it is not uncommon for cricketers to be good golfers, and there are lots of lawyers who end up in amateur or professional acting roles. For cricketers, batting and hitting a golf ball require broadly similar skills. For the lawyers, if you can get up and think on your feet in front of a judge and jury, performing in front of an audience is a piece of cake! The challenge for the career change person is to look into their past working life and pull out all the knowledge, skills, abilities and attitudes that may be able to make a contribution to the new career.

The career changer has to reshape their past working lives to show their accumulated experience in a new light that maximises the similarity between them and the job.

SALES REPRESENTATIVES

Deci Co. in Glasgow requires Sales Representatives to expand their sales to corporate clients. While experience in the printing industry is not essential, a proven sales and service ability in the above market would be a clear advantage. You should be highly motivated and focused on building a client base. You understand that success comes from building relationships with customers and tenaciously developing and promoting printing solutions to a wide industry client base. This position suits a practical results-driven achiever who seeks an attractive remuneration package.

Please send CV to:

Douglas Giles, Giles Recruitment
PO Box 73
Glasgow
G73 2PU

The 'before' CV

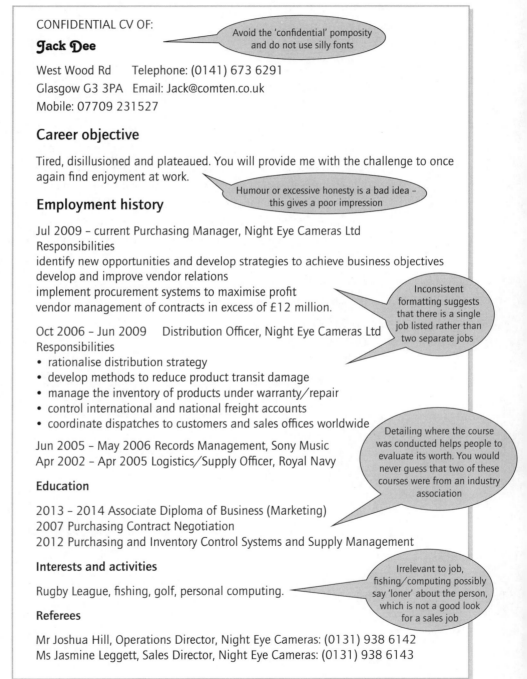

CONFIDENTIAL CV OF:

𝔍ack 𝔇ee

Avoid the 'confidential' pomposity and do not use silly fonts

West Wood Rd   Telephone: (0141) 673 6291
Glasgow G3 3PA   Email: Jack@comten.co.uk
Mobile: 07709 231527

Career objective

Tired, disillusioned and plateaued. You will provide me with the challenge to once again find enjoyment at work.

Humour or excessive honesty is a bad idea – this gives a poor impression

Employment history

Jul 2009 – current Purchasing Manager, Night Eye Cameras Ltd
Responsibilities
identify new opportunities and develop strategies to achieve business objectives
develop and improve vendor relations
implement procurement systems to maximise profit
vendor management of contracts in excess of £12 million.

Inconsistent formatting suggests that there is a single job listed rather than two separate jobs

Oct 2006 – Jun 2009   Distribution Officer, Night Eye Cameras Ltd
Responsibilities
• rationalise distribution strategy
• develop methods to reduce product transit damage
• manage the inventory of products under warranty/repair
• control international and national freight accounts
• coordinate dispatches to customers and sales offices worldwide

Jun 2005 – May 2006 Records Management, Sony Music
Apr 2002 – Apr 2005 Logistics/Supply Officer, Royal Navy

Education

2013 – 2014 Associate Diploma of Business (Marketing)
2007 Purchasing Contract Negotiation
2012 Purchasing and Inventory Control Systems and Supply Management

Detailing where the course was conducted helps people to evaluate its worth. You would never guess that two of these courses were from an industry association

Interests and activities

Rugby League, fishing, golf, personal computing.

Irrelevant to job, fishing/computing possibly say 'loner' about the person, which is not a good look for a sales job

Referees

Mr Joshua Hill, Operations Director, Night Eye Cameras: (0131) 938 6142
Ms Jasmine Leggett, Sales Director, Night Eye Cameras: (0131) 938 6143

The 'after' CV

Jack Dee

Address: West Wood Rd
Glasgow G3 3PA
Email: Terry@comten.co.uk

Telephone: (0141) 673 6291
Mobile: (07709) 231527

Career objective

I am keen to utilise my selling and customer service skills in a representative role that focuses on building relationships with existing customers, as well as translating opportunities into new accounts.

Skills, experience and personal attributes

Customer service

By developing better relationships with vendors and suppliers I have been successful in generating significant improvements to customer service at Night Eye Cameras Ltd. I introduced a system to support the introduction of new products including better documentation, customer training and a customer hotline to deal with any product queries quickly. I believe that the key to good customer service is servicing existing clients as if you were trying to win their business for the first time. It is important to understand what is most important to them and then to address this need.

Selling skills

In previous roles I have been responsible for identifying new opportunities and developing strategies to turn these into reality. In my purchasing roles I have been given a unique insight into customer needs from their perspective. I understand the importance of their needs being identified, turning product features into customer benefits and closing a deal that benefits both supplier and customer.

Highly motivated

I have achieved significant cost savings and efficiency improvements in previous positions and look forward to the opportunity to do the same thing for Deci Co. Promotions in previous positions have been the result of these efforts being recognised and rewarded.

Education

Associate Diploma of Business (Marketing)

2013 – 2014   Panorama College, Pollok

Short courses

Purchasing and Inventory Control Systems and Supply Management

2012   Institute of Purchasing Professionals

Purchasing Contract Negotiation

2007   Institute of Purchasing Professionals

Employment history

Jul 2009 – current   Purchasing Manager, Night Eye Cameras Ltd

Responsibilities

Identify new opportunities and develop strategies to achieve business objectives, develop and improve vendor relations, implement procurement systems to maximise profit, vendor management of contracts in excess of £12 million.

Achievements

- Annual six-digit savings in material expenditure

- Successful negotiation of supply contracts with over ten offshore vendors

- Implemented cost-reduction techniques making Scotland-based manufacturing more cost-effective than overseas contract assemblers

- Implemented a successful vendor assistance programme targeting new product support

- Optimised storage facilities with the adoption of improved stock handling methods.

Oct 2006 – Jul 2009   Distribution Officer, Night Eye Cameras Ltd

Responsibilities

Rationalise distribution strategy, develop methods to reduce product transit damage, manage the inventory of products under warranty/repair, control international and national freight accounts, coordinate dispatches to customers and sales offices worldwide.

Achievements

- Consolidated freight services, resulting in an increase of corporate bargaining power
- Reduced transit damage to under 0.5%.

| Jun 2005 – May 2006 | Records Management, Sony Music |
| Apr 2002 – April 2005 | Logistics/Supply Officer, Royal Navy |

Referees

Mr Joshua Hill, Operations Director, Night Eye Cameras: (0131) 938 6142
Ms Jasmine Leggett, Sales Director, Night Eye Cameras: (0131) 938 6143

An alternative makeover

Jack's CV is an ideal case for putting most of the evidence in the competency statements and trimming down the information in the less relevant experience. Here is an alternative makeover to consider.

Jack Dee

Address: West Wood Rd
Glasgow G3 3PA
Email: J.Dee@comten.co.uk

Telephone: (01773) 588888
Mobile: 07709231527

Career objective

I am keen to utilise the customer service expertise, client relationship building skills and ability to identify new business opportunities demonstrated in my previous purchasing roles to move into a target-driven representative role in sales.

Skills, experience and personal attributes

Business acumen

By developing better relationships with vendors and suppliers I have been successful in generating significant improvements to customer service at Night

Career objective

Eye Cameras Ltd. I introduced a system to support the introduction of new products including better documentation, customer training and a customer hotline to deal with any product queries quickly. This led to increased customer satisfaction ratings and greater customer loyalty.

Business development and sales

In previous roles I have been responsible for identifying new opportunities and developing strategies to turn these into reality. At Night Eye Cameras I spotted opportunities to reduce costs in our Scottish manufacturer. I persuaded them to implement these improvements, making them competitive with overseas providers. This led to subsequent savings in administration and logistics within Night Eye. I successfully renegotiated contracts with ten offshore vendors to gain unprecedented discounts leading to cost savings of 15%.

Highly motivated and results driven

In all of my roles I have sought to improve efficiency and save costs. At Night Eye I optimised our storage facilities and stock handling procedures to reduce delays in order processing leading to better customer service. I was promoted to my current role after consolidating our freight services, resulting in an increase of corporate bargaining power and reduced transit damage to under 0.5%.Employment history

Jul 2009–current Purchasing Manager, Night Eye Cameras Ltd
Identify new opportunities and develop strategies to achieve business objectives, develop and improve vendor relations, implement procurement systems to maximise profit, vendor management of contracts in excess of £12 million.

Oct 2006–Jul 2009 Distribution Officer, Night Eye Cameras Ltd
Rationalise distribution strategy, develop methods to reduce product transit damage, manage the inventory of products under warranty/repair, control international and national freight accounts, coordinate dispatches to customers and sales offices worldwide.

Jun 2005 – May 2006 Records Management, Sony Music

Apr 2002 – April 2005 Logistics/Supply Officer, Royal Navy

Education

2013–2014 Associate Diploma of Business (Marketing),

Panorama College, Pollok

Short courses

2012 Purchasing and Inventory Control Systems and Supply
        Management, Institute of Purchasing Professionals

2007 Purchasing Contract Negotiation, Institute of Purchasing

Referees

Mr Joshua Hill, Operations Director, Night Eye Cameras: (0131) 938 6142
Ms Jasmine Leggett, Sales Director, Night Eye Cameras: (0131) 938 6143

Career change checklist

- Name, full address, telephone numbers, up-to-date email address
- Believable competency statements backed up with evidence linking your old career competences to the new required competences
- Evidence of sustained achievement
- Evidence of energy and enthusiasm
- Emphasis on achievements and results
- Details of work experience and voluntary work emphasising information
- relevant to the new career and omitting industry specific jargon unlikely to be meaningful to the recruiter
- Full educational qualifications
- Snappy career statement
- Printed on high-quality paper or emailed in PDF format
- Two referees (whom you have already approached), including full contact details

CHAPTER 17

Tricky CV issues

Dealing with prejudice

One of the most commonly asked questions about writing a CV is what to do about bias. This is a really difficult one to answer, and we are sure there is no one correct way to go about this. Rather, you need to reflect on your own values when deciding what to do.

The first thing to say is that there is a lot of it about. The second thing to say very quickly is that, for some groups, things are getting a bit better.

Bias exists in all forms and includes, but is not limited to:

- ethnicity
- gender
- sexuality
- marital status
- religious beliefs
- age
- health
- weight
- height
- beauty
- perceived social class
- address
- clothes

- political beliefs
- education
- physical disability.

Study after study has shown that recruiters are biased either deliberately or unconsciously, and (guess what!) the most successful job candidates are young, white, attractive, middle-class, well-educated males, followed by their female counterparts.

A recent study we conducted showed that people presented with CVs containing photographs of the candidates were more likely to be influenced by the candidate's looks if the candidate was female. For men and women, the less attractive candidates were less likely to be short-listed.

Strategies for dealing with this are very complex and personal.

One approach is to conceal information that may prejudice your chances of being short-listed. To some, we know, this can be extremely insulting. They are justifiably proud of themselves and see concealment of facts as playing up to the bigots. This is perfectly understandable, and that is where personal choice comes in.

Health, physical characteristics, age and marital status are information about yourself we suggest you generally omit. These are irrelevant to most jobs.

If you do decide to conceal your gender, ethnicity or sexuality on your CV, be sure that you do so consistently. If you have a French-sounding surname such as Depardieu, and you have mentioned that you speak fluent French, you will be assumed to be at least of French descent.

Some studies demonstrate that ethnic identity will be judged on name alone. If prejudices exist these are applied regardless of whether the participant identifies with the culture represented or not. So while you have a choice about whether or not to attach a photo, there is really no choice about whether to include your name.

If you conceal your gender by using initials rather than first names, stating that you attended Horsham Ladies' College is a dead giveaway!

Hobbies on your CV can be a giveaway, too (especially if you're branch secretary of the British Communist Party).

It is a sad fact that CVs that conceal some of the above items are more likely to be short-listed. While we despise this bias, it is reality, and it is up to you how you deal with it.

brilliant tip

If you really wish to include any of the above information and are worried about the impact it may have, it probably means you would not be happy working for the organisation in question in the first place.

It is also worth remembering that, just because the person who reads your CV may be prejudiced, this doesn't mean the people you will work with or for are also prejudiced. People working for recruitment consultants, or people working in human resources departments, may not be anything like the people you'll be working with.

A final point to make here is that, generally, the bigger the organisation, the more likely it is to have equal employment opportunity/affirmative action policies and officers. In theory, this should reduce problems of bias.

Gaps in career history

This is a difficult one, and when we studied several other commercially available CV guides we found that a couple advised that you explain gaps, a couple suggested you conceal gaps and a couple gave no advice!

So, we studied the impact of gaps of one year by giving recruiters a series of CVs, some of which had gaps that were explained, some that had unexplained gaps and some without gaps. We found that:

- gaps were noticed 50 per cent of the time by recruiters
- if the gap was noticed and was not explained, recruiters thought the applicant was less honest than the average

- if the gap was noticed and explained, recruiters thought the applicant was more honest than the average

- only one out of ten reasons for a gap ('full-time academic study') was seen as a positive by recruiters

- redundancy, both voluntary and involuntary, is still seen poorly by recruiters, despite what some commentators say

- if the word 'caring' (as in 'caring for an ill parent') appeared in the explanation of a gap, the recruiters assumed the candidate was female.

Our advice is to explain any gaps – provided you have a good enough story to tell.

brilliant tip

Remember, the CV is often used at the interview stage to ask candidates questions. If the recruiters do not spot the gap during short-listing, it is likely they will spot it at the interview.

If you have had a gap in employment for a very negative reason, such as imprisonment, you may be tempted to conceal it. If the application format has explicitly asked you to reveal any conviction, be careful about failure to disclose this information as it could jeopardise your employment if discovered. If in doubt as to whether this information needs to be revealed or not, seek advice, or get a friend to call the recruiter and ask for their guidance. However, you must never tell untruths in a CV. Lying about any aspect of your life during recruitment can be grounds for dismissal if uncovered. For more information on seeking employment with a criminal record contact Nacro (the crime reduction charity): **helpline@nacro.org.uk**.

If you are forced to have many unexplained gaps in your work history, then it is almost certain that you should use the functional CV. This format concentrates on skills and abilities and not on dates and times. Think back to the CV see-saw (Chapter 6). This CV emphasises the right-hand side of the see-saw.

Electronic CVs

The development in electronic communication has brought about many new possibilities. We can now advertise jobs on the internet, apply for jobs on the internet, submit our CVs to sites on the internet, email our CVs directly to employers, and we can set up personal webpages on the internet.

Recruiters can now electronically scan CVs, in order to do all the screening automatically. Yes, it is now possible that only a computer will read your CV!

Tips for CVs that will be scanned

All scanners work on the same principles. They are looking for key words or phrases that have been programmed into the computer.

The words that companies scan for are often nouns and proper nouns, for instance, 'Excel' or 'Word' or 'automatic payroll systems'.

If you think it likely that your CV will be scanned electronically, this may be the time to use jargon or specialist language – provided that it is meaningful to people in your own industry. For instance, you might use terms like:

- AI (artificial intelligence)
- HTML (Hyper Text Markup Language – a computer programming language)
- ROI (return on investment)
- WYSIWYG (what you see is what you get).

brilliant tip

Repeat nouns and proper nouns used in the job ad to increase the chances that scanners will pick up on them.

Format is also important for scanned CVs. Layout should be clear and easy for a scanner to read.

The use of headings can assist here – remember, where you might otherwise refrain from using a heading for fear of insulting your reader's intelligence, computers do not have feelings, so spell everything out for them!

Headings such as the following may be useful:

- Experience
- Education
- Qualifications
- Work history
- Positions held
- Affiliations
- References.

The computer programs used to read your CV are becoming increasingly sophisticated, and therefore it is a canny idea to use some keywords to describe your personal qualities here too. Look back at the typical qualities that companies look for and, of course, the ones you have deduced from your detective work.

Words that might be useful here are:

- leader or leadership
- communicator
- sociable
- motivated
- energetic
- excellent
- outstanding
- skilled
- intelligent
- team player
- team-focused
- outgoing
- persuasive

- dependable
- reliable.

Unusual fonts are never a good idea, especially when the CV might be scanned. Use Times, Times New Roman, Optima, Verdana, Tahoma, Arial or Palatino. The font size should be in the normal letter range of 10 to 14 point. Although earlier we suggested that a 20-point font for your name looks good, err on the side of caution if you think the CV is going to be scanned, and use a smaller font.

If you include telephone numbers, list each one on separate lines, as a scanner may read numbers on the same line as one number. This will cause difficulties for people who subsequently look you up on a computer database when they want to contact you.

Underlining can make scanning more difficult, and doesn't look appealing generally, so desist.

The layout also affects the number of characters per line. In general, you should ensure that you do not have more than 70 to 80 characters per line, or scanning programs may reproduce the CV with some lines wrapped around onto the next line, causing the formatting to be messed up.

Avoid using columns like a newspaper. Start each new piece of information on a new line, fully aligned to the left. Look back to Chapter 9, where we compared different layouts. The best layout for a machine-readable CV is CV 1 (see page 120).

Do not put lines, pictures or graphics on your CV, as these will confuse the scanner.

Finally, if you are mailing your CV to the employer using conventional mail, try to avoid folding it up to put it in an envelope. Put the CV in an appropriately sized envelope, and preferably one that has a reinforced cardboard back, to help prevent creasing.

Emailing CVs

As an alternative to mailing your CV, most employers now are happy to receive them electronically via email. This can speed up the recruitment process and can save money too.

There are a few pointers to take into consideration.

As with scanned CVs, you should keep to a maximum of 70 to 80 characters per line. Any more and you risk losing the formatting.

You should send the CV as an attachment. Do not be tempted to copy and paste it into the body of the email – you will lose most of the formatting. Remember, even though you may have a fancy email program that allows you to include formatting and graphics in the message body, the majority of email programs around do not allow this, and all you will do is send an unintelligible mess to your prospective employer.

If you do decide to send your CV electronically, the safest format to use is probably a PDF file. This preserves your formatting and layout faithfully unlike a Word document in which the settings can change on different computers. Most modern word processing software allows you to save or export your document as a PDF file and most computers come with free PDF viewers.

brilliant tip

CVs sent electronically may not be as secure as those sent by conventional mail. If your application is very sensitive, this point needs to be considered.

Email is an easy and quick way to send things off. Resist the temptation to compose your CV and mail it off immediately. Many of us have had that sinking feeling just after we have hit the send button that we have sent the wrong version, sent it to the wrong person, or have included a glaring error.

brilliant tip

Always print off a copy of your CV and have someone else read it before mailing or emailing it.

Online CVs

Some recruitment sites allow you to create an online CV to use in a number of different applications. They may charge employers to look through their database of CVs. There are a couple of issues with this approach. One is confidentiality. How do you know who has access to your details? Always check before uploading. The other issue is customisability. In this book we encourage you to tailor your CV to the needs of a specific job/role you are applying for. If you upload one online CV, this will have to do for every job you go for. You might be alright if every job is identical.

This one-size-fits-all problem applies to a LinkedIn profile. Employers are increasingly checking out potential candidates' profiles on the LinkedIn social networking site before considering them for interview. LinkedIn is a very useful networking and job hunting tool, and it's a good idea to be on there, but make sure your profile is honed to attract the right kind of employers.

For some jobs, having a personal webpage can be a real advantage. An obvious example is if you are a web designer. You can show off your talents. Personal webpages are also used by programmers, photographers, graphic designers and the like to showcase a portfolio of their work to potential employers.

Personal webpages demonstrate the remarkable things that people will reveal about themselves that they'd never dream of including in a professional document.

Employers generally are not interested in 'meeting the babies', 'looking at my boat' or 'sitting in my front room'. If you intend to set up your webpage as a substitute CV, then you must apply the same levels of professionalism as you would to a conventional CV. The key difference with a webpage CV is that you can include far more information, provided it is appropriately indexed and the site can be navigated easily. However, the initial key pages of the site should convey all the critical information of a conventional CV. Use the extra potential of a website for additional optional information in links that employers can choose to follow.

Website CVs become public documents, which potentially can be accessed by anyone, including your current boss. Do you really want all your personal details laid out for everyone to see?

Some valuable further resources on web-based CVs and the like are offered in Chapter 18.

What are the steps in the recruitment process?

There are no hard and fast rules about how people recruit, but the steps described below are fairly typical, though some firms will do things in a different order and some organisations will skip certain sections.

CV screening

This is what this book is all about. In this stage, recruiters narrow down the number of applicants by reading their CVs.

Sometimes this screening may involve a brief telephone interview with the recruiter before you are asked to submit a CV (and sometimes this telephone screening occurs after the recruiter has read your CV – there are no fixed rules on these stages).

Psychological testing or assessment centres

Some of the larger recruiters may ask you to complete an online psychometric test before or after submitting an application. This tests for specific aptitudes such as numerical or verbal reasoning.

You may be asked to attend an assessment session, which could last between one hour and five hours (you will be told in advance).

You will be asked to complete pencil and paper or computer-based tests designed to test your intelligence, personality, or particular skills such as reading and numeracy.

Interview

The interview stage may consist of one face-to-face interview, or it could involve a whole series of interviews on one day with different people or over a period of time.

A face-to-face interview is the most common and involves you being asked a series of questions about you and your thoughts on the job.

Panel interviews have several people at once interviewing you. Do not be nervous – these are often fairer than the one-to-one variety.

The questions you get asked here might be prompted by your CV or the results of your psychological testing. When preparing your CV, think ahead to the interview. What achievements on your CV would you love the opportunity to talk about during the interview because they are relevant and impressive?

Offer or rejection

About a week to four weeks after the deadline for applications closes, you are likely to hear whether you are being invited for an interview. Unfortunately, employers are often slower to send out rejection letters, or don't send them at all.

You can expect to hear the outcome of an interview a bit more promptly. Often people have arrived home from the interview to find a voicemail message for them saying 'Congratulations!'

If you are offered the job, take your time to let things sink in before accepting. Most employers will give you a little time to think things over, but do not expect them to give you very long. Often there is a second good candidate who they do not wish to lose, should you turn them down.

If you are unlucky enough to be rejected, then join the club! You are in the overwhelming majority. Nearly everybody has been turned down for a job at some time or another.

brilliant tip

If you are rejected, do not write an abusive letter or make an abusive phone call to the recruiter or employer – this is highly unprofessional and will risk your reputation with that employer and other prospective employers who get wind of your behaviour.

Sometimes, and we stress sometimes, some employers are willing to provide feedback to you if it is asked for in a polite, positive manner, and the purpose is to assist you in strengthening future job applications. However, many employers rightly fear that prolonging the dialogue may expose them to legal action or might mislead the candidate. Sometimes it really is the luck of the draw.

You might be able to increase your chances of getting useful feedback by asking specific questions. 'Were there any particular competencies that I failed to provide convincing evidence for?' might be more likely to get a response than 'Can you give me any feedback?'

Do I include referees and, if so, who should they be?

There is mixed advice from recruiters on this topic. Our preference is to include referee contact details as the last item on your CV. The reason for saying this rather than 'Referees available on request' is that it makes it easier for the employer. They do not have to make an extra call to get names and addresses. We also wonder how many people who have put 'Referees available on request' have panicked when asked for them because they have not bothered to work out who the referees would be.

Known to us personally are at least 10 examples of candidates who have unwittingly continued to use a referee who has written extremely negative things about them. On other occasions, it is clear that the candidate has failed to ask the permission of a referee in advance when comments such as 'Last time I had contact with him he was unemployed in Cardiff' are made. This brings us to our next brilliant tip.

brilliant tip

Always ensure that you know your referee well, and that they are happy to write or say something positive about you.

Not only should you ask the referee's permission, you should treat them with respect. That means you should inform them what sort of job you are applying for (you don't want a referee to express surprise on the phone). Do not abuse your referee by making them respond to hundreds of different employers that you have indiscriminately applied to.

The best referees are people who have supervised you in your recent jobs, especially the one you currently hold. Not only does this look more impressive, it tells the employer that you are not at loggerheads with your current supervisor. If this is not practical (because you are trying to maintain confidentiality), try using someone who has previously supervised you and has left the company or now works in a different area. Whatever you decide, remember that it is important to have as recent a referee as possible, since this is most likely to relate to the position you are applying for.

If you cannot get a reference from a current or recent employer or, alternatively, the job ad has asked for 'character references', you need to approach some other people. This is going to cause outrage among some readers, but there are some people who are more suitable than others. In general, people in 'professional' jobs are generally seen as 'good' referees:

- lawyers
- judges
- teachers
- lecturers
- police officers
- government councillors
- company directors (but the company needs to be respectable)
- senior managers.

Here are a few horror stories and perhaps some urban myths:

- 'the best way of getting rid of a poor employee is to provide them with a brilliant reference'
- candidates who invent their own references
- candidates who use relatives with different names as referees.

We genuinely have seen a CV where the candidate had included a statement from a referee, who was his best friend's mother, and that was dated more than 14 years earlier. And another where a candidate using a false name and address of a referee turned out to be himself using a fake Scottish accent. Unfortunately for him, the accent wore off as the reference progressed and he said some unbelievably good things about himself. Needless to say, neither of these applicants got the job!

Do I include a photograph?

There are some things we strongly suggest you 'conceal', and this especially applies to photographs. Do not include one for a number of reasons:

1 We did a survey of a large recruitment firm's archive of CVs and could not find a single photograph attached to a successful CV.

2 In another more recent survey we carried out, of over 625 CVs sent to a recruitment firm, only 7 included photographs. Interestingly, six of these candidates were male. There were twice as many males as females, but the males were six times more likely to include a photograph than females. Furthermore, not one of the candidates who attached a photograph was short-listed, compared with 17 per cent of the candidates who did not include a photograph.

3 Not everyone looks like a supermodel, or photographs like one.

4 Sending a photograph is telling employers: 'I want to be judged on my looks and not on job-relevant characteristics.'

5 In another recently completed study, we compared identical CVs that included a photograph of a person who was independently judged to be attractive or unattractive. The results were depressingly inevitable: attractive candidates were judged more suitable for the job and were more likely to be short-listed compared with unattractive candidates. This goes for men as well as women.

Interestingly, this beauty bias was more evident for women applying for a clerical position than for women applying for a higher-status legal position. We also found that it did not matter whether the job involved seeing clients or customers – attractive candidates were still more highly rated.

What are recruiters thinking when they read CVs?

We have extensively researched this question and it is clear that certain themes emerge. Below we provide a list of comments that have been collected in a series of systematic CV experiments. The comments all come from professional recruitment personnel and human resources officers.

Recent research shows that recruiters make all sorts of decisions just based on the CV. For example, most recruiters believe they can confidently rate how smart you are, how conscientious you are, your interpersonal skills, as well as any job-related knowledge, just by examining your CV[1]. Other studies show that recruiters could infer whether or not someone was extroverted from their CV content with some accuracy but not other personality characteristics such as agreeableness, neuroticism, openness and conscientiousness[2]. Even when their predictions were not correct, these initial assessments were carried through the decision-making process.

Read through these statements – we believe they give you a unique insight into how recruiters think about the CV screening process. Notice how the comments vary from recruiter to recruiter.

Notice also that much of what they are saying is reflected in the advice we have given you in this book. Our advice comes from studies conducted with these professionals and augmented by our professional experience.

All the statements in this section are direct quotes taken from interviews and surveys with professional recruiters. The comments refer to CVs we asked the recruiters to read and screen as if they were taking part in a typical recruitment exercise. We asked recruiters which CVs they liked and why, the problems with the CVs they did not like, and how they came to make their decisions.

---

[1] Chen, C.-C., Huang, Y.-M., Lee, M.-I. (2011). 'Test of a model linking applicant résumé information and hiring recommendations.' *International Journal of Selection and Assessment*, 19(4), 374–387.

[2] Cole, M. S., Feild, H. S., Giles, W. F., and Harris, S. G. (2009). 'Recruiters' inferences of applicant personality based on résumé screening: Do paper people have a personality?' *Journal of Business Psychology*, 24, 5–18.

What do recruiters like most in CVs?

The three factors they appreciated most were:

1 Relevant experience

2 Layout

3 Qualifications.

▶ brilliant example

Here are five examples of recruiters' comments about CVs they rated highly because of relevant experience:

1 Clear employment history, attributes clearly organised. CV very well put together and quite clear.

2 Clear, direct description of experience in relation to the competencies described.

3 Computer skills, people skills, experience dealing with managers. A team player, thorough, ambitious.

4 Relevant work experience. Excellent mathematical skills. Strong track record of experience.

5 Scope of experience, ability to work and co-ordinate job role unsupervised.

Now see why layout is important in these comments from our team of recruiters:

- Good, clear layout, highlighted awards.

- Clear, well-ordered, logical, easy to read. Stable and relevant employment. Excellent academic qualifications.

- Responds to specific needs in the ad. Very well presented, clearly described details of experience and outcomes.

- Bold headings, logical layouts (qualifications should be on page one). Tasks, duties, position all very clear.

- Highlights those experiences most relevant to the job. Phrasing and format gave strong impression of qualities relevant to the position.

The recruiters responded to CVs emphasising qualifications in this way:

- Tertiary qualifications. Work experience relates to job requirements. Business information skills. Relevant extra-curricular activities. High level of analysis and motivation. Layout of CV.

- Major assignments and rewards. Length of time employed and duties successfully undertaken while employed. Initiative in having own business.

- Degree project work (results on paper). Education. Work history. Marketing knowledge.

- Relevant work experience, mix of administration, customer service, analysis. Relevant study/qualifications exposed to systems. Easy to read, well laid out.

- Combination of qualifications, communication skills, expansion on experience, evidence of drive, energy, appropriate focus and experience.

What do recruiters dislike in a CV?

Here are five examples of comments made by recruiters about CVs they did not like, starting with relevant experience:

1 Very little experience (in time spent), too theoretical, that is, skills are demonstrated in education, not in workforce. University results (although comprehensive) show weaknesses in areas of most importance.

2 Previous employment history does not exactly mix with the role being applied for.

3 Academic, little experience. Lacks ambition and enthusiasm, no continuity of employment.

4 Not as much relevant experience although shows initiative through own business. Layout of CV a little difficult to read.

5 Mainly research experience. Concerns about how applicant would go in the real world.

Poor layout can leave a poor impression on recruiters, as these examples show:

- Layout of CV terrible. Information too difficult to make sense of.
- Format annoying. Information irrelevant to this job.
- CV all over the place. No logic, difficult to follow. Can't be bothered persevering to find information.
- Little reference to position description. Poor point size. Bad layout with two columns. Very busy CV.
- Too much information per page. No logical sequence. Text is very small, though information is very good.

Recruiters looking for qualifications react very negatively when they're not there. For example:

- No demonstration or examples of the required/desired competencies. Nothing outstanding that would lead to thinking there may be special qualities.
- Does not show academic results. Poor level of detail on positions held.
- Job advertisement is looking for someone with a strong desire to pursue a sales career. This applicant has been 'back room'.
- Limited experience while working in buying field. Comparing CVs, this one has the least experience (in uni and work).
- Leaves me with the feeling that I need to be informed of more detail to appropriately gauge the candidate's suitability.

How do recruiters use job competencies to discern a good 'fit'?

A study in 2007[3] asked recruiters to independently rate a number of CVs. The study concluded that the recruiters used a complex interaction of

---

[3] Cole, M. S., Rubin, R. S., Field, H. S. and Giles, W. F., 'Recruiters' perceptions and use of applicant résumé information: screening the recent graduate', *Applied Psychology: An international review*, 2007, 56 (2), 319–343.

evidence from academic qualifications, work experience and extra-curricular activities to make a decision. Recruiters try to balance strengths in some areas to compensate for weaknesses in others. Using competency statements increases the likelihood that recruiters will be able to identify evidence from all three areas that are most relevant.

In a recent study we looked at the effectiveness of including competency statements in CVs. Taking a sales analyst's position as an example, we asked a team of professional recruiters to list, in order of importance, the 10 competencies they most valued and comment on them. We then counted the number of times all the recruiters mentioned those competencies in their comments.

The result in the following table reflects that count, showing the competencies the recruiters regarded as important for the position of sales analyst. (If we carried out this exercise for a different position, for example a laboratory technician, the results would be very different.)

	Number of times mentioned
Communication skills	31
Numerical skills	26
Planning and organising	20
Market knowledge	19
Achievement orientation	17
Initiative with responsibility	16
Problem solving	11
Motivation	11
Energy	6
Tenacity	3

As you can see, an overall pattern emerges suggesting that communication skills and numerical skills were regarded as the most important. This supports the idea that recruiters build up their own opinions of which competencies are ideal for a particular position, in this case a sales analyst.

Here are some samples of why the different recruiters thought the different competencies were important for the sales analyst position.

Most valued competencies	Recruiters' comments
Achievement orientation	This is needed to keep up the level of motivation and move from an analysis role to a sales-oriented role in the future. Applicant needs to be an achiever with an understanding of the business, driven to assist account managers.
Achievement orientation with communication skills	Any sales role needs a track record of demonstrable success. Communication skills are critical in sales.
Achievement orientation with initiative and responsibility	The applicant needs drive, ability and tenacity to meet goals. A graduate should be questioned about the responsibility to undertake activities and see them through.
Achievement orientation with numerical skills	This new position depends on achieving results in increased sales/market share. Key technical skill is the ability to collect and process relevant data. If this was not applicable, then communication skills would be ranked highest. This sales analyst role is to provide crucial information to assist in final sales. It requires extensive analysis.
Achievement orientation with planning and organising skills	The successful candidate must be goal oriented to handle this position which will need planning and organising skills because it is a new role.
Communication skills	This is the most valued competency because you can achieve anything with good communicators. There is internal and external liaison involved. Analysts need to get their conclusion across to their managers as well as clients. Customers demand excellent communication skills and a commitment to deliver.
Communication skills with initiative and responsibility	Written, oral and listening skills form the key to succeeding in this role. The role needs a person who will work diligently without constant supervision.
Communication skills with market knowledge	This role requires collective market/product information and collating in a form that can be used by clients. Experience in a team environment is required to deal with many parties, and to distribute information. It's clearly important for the applicant to have some idea of, and background in, the market area involved.
Communication with problem-solving skills	The concerns of customers will always need a high level of problem solving.
Communication with numerical skills	Ability to communicate with a wide range of people, know how the industry operates and interpret requirements for analysis is imperative.

Most valued competencies	Recruiters' comments
Communication with planning and organising skills	Verbal ability to liaise with customers/peers/managers essential. Excellent written communication required in user-friendly presentation of data/results. Applicant will need to be a self-starter who is able to plan and organise own schedule.
Energy	Customer and account manager service will be affected directly by the energy and 'urgency' of the person who fills this role.
Initiative with responsibility	The role needs a person who takes their workload seriously and responsibly and creates efficiency through reduced human resource management. The applicant must be able to take on responsibility, empower people, and be able to take knocks and bounce back.
Initiative with responsibility and achievement orientation	Initiative and responsibility need to be established as priorities otherwise all else is affected. Respect, awareness and commitment are paramount, particularly within a team environment.
Initiative with responsibility and problem-solving skills	As the role reports to several managers, the applicant needs to be a self-starter. The role is analytically focused with the need to collect data and work through it piece by piece, as well as see the big picture, to get results.
Initiative with responsibility and tenacity	This person needs less direction, and will produce a higher work output of greater quality than others.
Market knowledge	The ability to monitor products from their own and a competitive situation is essential to the business performance. Important to understand what the products are, and where they sit in the marketplace.
Market knowledge with communication skills	Proof of efforts to understand and research market areas is essential. Manner is as important as ability and aptitude.
Market knowledge with planning and organising	The role requires a good understanding of the market to perform the job to the best of their ability.
Motivation	Enthusiasm will allow even the least competent to shine.
Motivation with energy	These competencies are by far the most important. Without them, you will only ever be employed as an assistant sales analyst. These competencies are far in excess of the need for the candidate to be a graduate.
Motivation with initiative and responsibility	To provide constant and accurate reports to both customers and colleagues.

▶

Most valued competencies	Recruiters' comments
Numerical skills	You can't analyse if you can't do the sums. The role involves evaluation of sales forecasts versus actuals. Without good numerical analysis skills in this area, the business could lose sales.
Numerical skills with communication	The role requires numerical reasoning and understanding. Liaison with account managers, marketplace providers and users has to be clear and concise. This role includes analysis of data, sales forecasts and monitoring of pricing, as well as liaison, report preparation and promotion strategies.
Planning and organising	The applicant needs good skills in this area to cope with the volume and variety of work, and juggle the number of people to report to.
Planning and organising with communication skills	Given the number of projects involved in this role and account manager liaison, the ability to plan and organise oneself is critical. The need to liaise with customers, gather information and determine their needs makes communication skills critical.
Planning and organising with numerical skills	The role involves organising and planning data collection and collation. Statistical skills in analysing results are essential. There are many reports and analytical work required on sales and marketing issues.
Planning and organising with problem-solving skills	This competency requires an ability to collate and deliver information to others, a need to ascertain and analyse data and evaluate various information.
Problem solving	Good problem-solving skills are necessary to support the numerical skills in evaluating and reporting market information. The role requires exceptional analytical ability.
Tenacity	People with tenacity are more likely to succeed than people who rely on any other individual competency.

As a contrast to the information given on the previous pages, we asked recruiters to list which of 10 different competencies was their least valued when recruiting somebody into the position of a sales analyst. And again, we counted the number of times they mentioned those competencies.

Competency	Number of times mentioned
Tenacity	34
Energy	33
Motivation	18
Market knowledge	9
Numerical skills	9
Problem solving	7
Initiative with responsibility	5
Achievement orientation	3
Communication skills	3
Planning and organising	1

Tenacity and energy were the least-valued competencies, followed by motivation. As was the case with the most-valued competencies, there was a strong opinion among the recruiters about the competencies that were not so important when preparing a CV for the sales analyst position.

Here are samples of the recruiters' comments about why they considered the various competencies were of little value.

Least valued competencies	Recruiters' comments
Achievement orientation	It is a backroom role and tends to be fairly process-oriented. Someone with a strong achievement orientation could become bored. This job does not require someone dominant in nature, as long as the job gets done within the time frame.
Communication skills	Person needs only to communicate internally at this stage with no client contact.
Energy	Energy is good but knowledge and efficiency are more important.
Initiative with responsibility	The applicants do not need as much of this because the position is a junior role.

Least valued competencies	Recruiters' comments
Market knowledge	This can be learned within months on the job. This is a graduate position and market knowledge would not be envisaged at this point.
Motivation	It is hard to tell this competency from CVs. It's needed but is not as important if goals are achieved. This person may be in the role for some time before promotion.
Numerical skills	All candidates should have this skill but other competencies rank more highly because part of the position relates to personal and other skills.
Planning and organising	The person will report to line managers so their responsibilities will be structured.
Problem solving	As the role is predominantly about producing reports from available data, this is not so important. The person would be under the wing of the sales manager and could develop this skill over time.
Tenacity	The position has been created to support the sales team. The candidates should not have to sell their services. Tenacity is useless when gathering information.

What do recruiters think about when they make decisions on CVs?

We asked two recruiters to think out loud when reading CVs. We recorded their thoughts on each, then grouped them according to the recruiter's short-listing decision.

Recruiter 1

Short-list decision	Recruiter's comments
CV rejected	• The CV includes mistaken terminology for 'customers'. • It is reasonably articulate but the applicant's grammar and communication skills are questionable. • The letter is too long. It taps into a few things about the role advertised, but focuses on marketing, not sales. • The applicant has an associate diploma instead of the necessary degree. • The applicant describes skills but the ad says the employer wants a demonstrated track record of achievement.

Short-list decision	Recruiter's comments
Unsure of CV at this stage	• It's too short and includes the applicant's marital status which is irrelevant and annoying. • I question their expectations, but I like the covering letter. • I'm not into what they think they're good at. I'd prefer to see what they have done. • I need to know how much business experience the applicant has had.
Interview granted, based on CV	• The candidate is able to demonstrate achievement. • The candidate worked all the way through university. • The CV demonstrates the candidate can manage a number of tasks. • The candidate lists financial forecasting, statistics, computer literacy. • It was an average CV, but the candidate has a good academic record.

Recruiter 2

Short-list decision	Recruiter's comments
CV rejected	• The CV is very hard to read. • There is too much school education. The university section is better laid out. • The only interesting thing in the CV is that the candidate 'speaks Japanese'. • There is nothing to support the candidate's original claims. • The candidate includes too much detail about extracurricular activities.
Unsure of CV at this stage	• The letter is quite interesting. The candidate starts off by saying what they do now and how they might relate to this job. • The candidate has retail experience, but the position doesn't need this. • Computer skills are important and the CV is well laid out. • The format of the CV is easy to scan.
Interview granted, based on CV	• In terms of key criteria, the competencies listed on the CV include achievement orientation and co-operation. • The interesting format makes me interested in the candidate.

How do recruiters decide between CVs in short-listing?

We asked recruiters to list the most common strategies they used in short-listing. Here are some of their answers.

Recruiters' strategies for short-listing CVs

---

1   The quality of written words and the structure of the covering letter.
2   Relevant experience.
3   Evidence of activities that indicate the nature of the applicant.

---

1   Academic qualifications are reviewed first, followed by a scan of the CV.
2   The structure of the covering letter is very important. Spelling mistakes are frowned upon.
3   Attention is focused on recent work experience.

Look for experience that approximates to what is required.

---

1   Match candidate's competencies with the position.
2   Match work experience with the position.
3   Check the candidate's tertiary qualifications.

Compare the candidate's experience and qualifications with their competencies.

---

1   Read the CV thoroughly.
2   Review the competencies.
3   Consider how the CV matches the competencies.
4   Re-evaluate the CV.
5   Make a decision on whether to reject it or recommend an interview.

The candidate's knowledge, experience and personal traits are compared with those required for the position.

---

1   Read the covering letter to evaluate the standard of writing and the ability to address advertisement requests.
2   Then scan CV to check education and experience requirements are met before reading the CV in depth to gauge the candidate's level of achievement, responsibility, team involvement, etc.

---

1   Qualifications, experience.
2   Evidence of literacy, expression, numeracy.
3   Potential, apparent focus.

Do recruiters eliminate CVs on one piece of information?

Again, here are a few sample responses from our recruiters.

Eliminating CVs on one piece of information

Yes. I eliminated one candidate because they had a poor covering letter and errors in the CV. This indicates lack of attention to detail and care.

Yes, because of spelling errors and poor grammar.

I look to include applicants rather than to eliminate them, but I finally rank and select the strongest candidates.

No, never.

I am definitely put off by typos, spelling and grammar errors. If you can't get it right when you're trying to make a good impression, what about every day?

Not really, it is a matter of one CV not being as good as another CV.

I look for the amount of information around achievements.

If a degree does not include a relevant major, I query real interest in the job and ability to perform. This, combined with very limited experience in the area, means they would not be considered for interview.

No. At least a couple of factors worked together.

Our professional recruiters tell you their one brilliant tip

Each recruiter was asked to nominate a single piece of advice for writers of CVs. Here are their brilliant tips.

✹ brilliant tips

- Make sure you have correct grammar with no spelling errors in the covering letter, and address the competencies required in the advertisement.

- The CV should contain a clear, concise and chronological format.

- Highlight the skills that meet the criteria and market and write with a positive attitude.

- Remember that you are marketing yourself so, while the integrity of the document is a must, the CV needs to present your best qualities and must detail your relevant skills and competencies.

- Include specifics like 'I achieved a 30 per cent increase in sales through the telesales initiative I introduced'.

- Do not overstate facts in the covering letter that can be obtained from reading the CV.

- Keep your CV short and to the point.

- Tailor the CV to suit the requirements of the ad and include achievements, not just duties, because these are what will sell you.

- Include examples to back up your competency statements.

- Follow the 4-S rule: keep your CV Simple, Structured, Succinct and Significant.

- Make sure your CV supports the advertised position criteria and the feel of the ad without waffling.

- Use a sharp covering letter and restrict the CV to two pages. Identify your strengths and weaknesses, if possible. Emphasise aspects of your background that have an immediate or apparent match with the job requirements.

- Put your major achievements and accomplishments in the CV, not just tasks and responsibilities.

- Avoid being repetitive in your CV.

- Use the active voice to describe what you have done in previous positions, and say why you want the job.

- Do your homework prior to applying. Find out about the company, obtain an annual report if available, find out what future projects the company might be involved with, who their clients are, who their competitors are.

- Clearly address the specific requirements called for so that the skills can be measured easily against the criteria, and then against those of the other applicants.
- Provide as much information as possible on work experience and tertiary education.

PART 4

Resource bank – useful ingredients and tips

In the last part of the book, we have provided you with some valuable resources to assist you in your CV preparation and job-seeking. Increasingly, job-seeking and job applications are being conducted via the internet, so we list some useful links. Given the nature of the internet, some of these inevitably will have changed in one way or another by the time you read this. However, we trust there are enough useful sites and links to get your net-surfing started!

CHAPTER 18

Finding out, finding others and being found: job searching for a new decade

n Chapter 1 we said your CV must sell you. Here we provide you with some strategies to help you find your target market and boost the selling power of your CV with a winning marketing plan. To do this effectively, use our CASTING model for your job-hunting strategies. Casting is a good word to describe job hunting because, in fishing, it means casting your net (or for us casting on the Net), and also it means hiring the right actors for the role, so it captures both the searching for the role and the landing of that role.

CASTING stands for:

Connect   with other people

Advertise   what you are good at, what you want, what you can offer

Share   information, tips, opportunities as well as your skill-set with others

Talk   to as many people as possible about what they do, what they need, and what problems they face

Impress   others by understanding their needs and promoting your achievements

Network   by systematically building and maintaining your network

Give   your time, knowledge, skills and experience to others, as well as your help and support

Connecting

The term 'get connected' is taken now to mean get on the Web, such has been the phenomenal growth of the internet. So Web strategies are a good place to start with our goal of connecting.

The internet is now a daily reality for the majority of people in the UK and this means it needs to figure as a central method for finding a job. According to the Office for National Statistics (**www.ons.gov.uk**) 21 million households in the UK (80 per cent) had internet access in 2009. In 2012, 33 million adults accessed the internet every day, more than double the 2006 figure of 16 million. Only 14 per cent of adults in the UK said they have never used a computer.

What all this means is that you should seriously consider putting your CV on the Web. There are lots of ways in which you can do this, but the most fundamental way of thinking about this is that every public document, comment or photograph you post on the Web, or your friends post naming you, becomes in effect part of your Web-based CV.

So ask yourself the question, 'Am I happy to let all this uncontrolled content represent me, or am I going to actively manage my Web-based reputation?'

Job boards

The easiest way to get your CV on the Web is to upload a copy of your CV to a job board, or complete the online forms that many of these sites provide. National newspapers (e.g. *The Guardian*, *The Daily Telegraph*) and recruitment firms (e.g. **Monster.co.uk**, **Executivesontheweb.com**, **Fish4jobs.co.uk**), along with some professional associations, all offer sites where you can upload an existing CV or fill out their forms and have one created for you. Do some homework first and determine the recruiters that will best suit your needs. The last thing you want to do is to end up in the crossfire when two competing agencies want to forward your award-winning résumé to a potential client. The more effort you put in to finding the right recruiter, the more you will distinguish yourself from other candidates by your motivation, initiative and proactivity. Start by having a look at their websites, newspaper ads, etc. to get a better understanding of the types and level of jobs they handle. Does the same recruiter handle the types of jobs you are most interested in? It might be worth a call to determine whether they are prepared to meet you in person.

This is a fantastic way of getting your CV working for you without the trouble of emailing or mailing copies to hundreds of possible employers.

In putting together CVs for job boards, try to include as many 'keywords' as possible. These are the words and phrases that recruiters are likely to enter in their search software when reading your CV or searching the CV database.

Keywords are the words and phrases you will have unearthed in the analysis and research steps (described in Chapters 3, 4 and 5).

When posting an online CV, you might have a range of different types of position you are interested in. This poses the dilemma of producing a very narrowly targeted résumé which risks being less than optimal for all jobs other than those in the target range, or producing a more generic CV that risks being too general for any position.

One way around this is to post multiple CVs that target the range of different roles you are interested in. You can do this either by putting different versions of your CV onto different job boards, or by creating multiple accounts with the same job board and posting the variations of your CV in different accounts.

Putting CVs on well-established and reputable job boards is straightforward, and these sites generally have great privacy provisions that restrict access to sensitive details like addresses and telephone numbers. Do check out the privacy settings and policies of any site on which you are considering posting your CV, to reduce the chances that your personal details get into the wrong hands.

Finally, if you are going to post your CV onto a job board, don't forget that you have done it, so you can remember to update it regularly with the latest version. Leaving old CVs hanging around in cyberspace is just asking for a potential employer to find it and perhaps make a decision based on out-of-date information. Keep a file with a list of places where you have posted the CV along with a URL and any user names and passwords you need to access the information.

Advertising and sharing

Social networking means interacting with other users of internet sites and services like Facebook, LinkedIn, Twitter and Foursquare. These sites provide resources that permit users to generate their own content and to share it with others in real time across the globe. It is like being on a conference telephone call simultaneously with over one billion other people (the number of active Facebook accounts at the time of writing).

While these sites originally were dominated by people sharing news, information and events from their private and social lives, increasingly social networking is being used by recruiters to glean information about job candidates and by job candidates to provide a showcase for their talents, to network with recruiters and to research job opportunities.

These sites provide an excellent opportunity to take your personal marketing strategy online. They also provide you with a way of taking control or at least partially managing the information that exists about you online. A survey by *Career Builder* in August 2009 found that 45 per cent of employers said they checked out applicants' social networking sites as part of their screening process. Do not expect that figure to decline; rather, it is not unreasonable to expect all employers will at the very least do a Google search on you before inviting you to interview.

Social networking site searches are increasingly being seen as another component in the recruitment process to augment candidate referee statements.

The biggest site currently (things change very fast in cyberspace) is Facebook. If you are actively searching for work, now is the time to lock down your personal Facebook account with the strictest privacy settings if it contains material likely to portray you in an unprofessional light. Into this category go weird hobbies, outspoken political or religious views, negative commentaries about work or work colleagues or companies, pictures depicting drunkenness, passion, illegality, or states of (semi-) nudity.

It is also a good time to do a Google and a Bing vanity search – a search on your name – to see what comes up. Material that you may have overlooked that could cause embarrassment includes: comments or reviews of books on Amazon; photos posted on sites such as Flickr or TwitPic; comments made in discussion news threads, blogs or newspapers. If any of these are likely to embarrass you, see whether there are mechanisms to remove the material.

One increasingly common problem is when other people, like old friends, post photographs on sites, for instance reunion sites, and then 'tag'(name) you. Much of this is harmless. There is relatively little you can do, but if the material is particularly worrying for you it may be worth contacting the person who posted it, or the website hosting it, to get it taken down.

Once you have cleared up as much negative marketing material as you can, you can focus more on the many benefits these sites offer to a motivated job hunter.

LinkedIn

LinkedIn is rapidly becoming an indispensible tool for the job hunter. Although some professions and industry sectors are better represented than others in LinkedIn members, an increasing number of employers and recruitment agencies are using it as their primary method to advertise vacancies and discover talented individuals.

If you are not currently on LinkedIn, you should probably consider it. If you are on LinkedIn, you should make sure your profile is optimised to attract the attention of recruiters in your area – and that it contains the appropriate key words to ensure that LinkedIn's search algorithms send the most appropriate vacancies in your direction. The advice we give in previous chapters of this book about targeting your CV and researching the jobs you want to apply for apply equally well to writing your LinkedIn profile.

However, aside from updating your profile, there are many other ways in which you can use LinkedIn to improve your job applications and increase your chances of success.

- Increase your network. The more people you are directly connected to, the wider your circle of indirect connections – the contacts of your contacts. This means you will have access to a wider range of people who may be able to provide you with inside information to help you refine your application.

- Read other people's profiles. There are two benefits of doing this. One is to see how successful people at your level present themselves. You could compare how different people emphasise their experience, attributes and achievements. The other benefit comes from looking at people in roles that you might aspire to in the future. You will probably pick up useful terminology and an idea of what aspects of your own experience to emphasise in order to demonstrate your future potential.

- Join relevant Groups. LinkedIn Groups allow people with similar professional interests to discuss relevant topics and share resources. They can be a great way of identifying potentially useful contacts in your chosen industry sector and raising your own professional profile. The topics discussed will also give you an insight into the needs of potential employers so that you can make sure your CV demonstrates abilities in the right areas.

Talking and impressing

Twitter is the social networking site that limits each message you send (called a 'tweet') to 140 characters. Due to its brevity, many people are dumbfounded as to why anyone would be interested in tweeting or, more weirdly, following the tweets of others. Other people wonder whether it is a service only for narcissists and celebrities – a 2009 survey by mobile phone maker INQ reported that Stephen Fry, Eddie Izzard, Russell Brand, two members of the McFly band and Jonathan Ross dominated the top 10 list of influential tweeters.

Don't be put off; Twitter is increasingly being used by clued-up job hunters to find jobs. Twitter can be useful to access job leads, meet people in your industry and establish yourself as an industry expert. So much so that our colleagues in the USA, Susan Britton Whitcomb, Chandlee Bryan and Deb Dib, have written a book on just this subject – *The Twitter Job Search Guide: Find a Job and Advance Your Career in Just 15 Minutes a Day* (Jist Works, 2010).

We particularly like their 'On the N.O.S.E.' model. Using this model, people can ensure their tweets are Newsworthy, On-brand, Strategic and Engaging.

Their point is, you don't use Twitter like some celebrities to say, 'I am sitting here watching the grass grow' but instead you can tweet, 'Just completed a course in customer service, loved it', or 'Just registered for Big Job Fair, hope to see you there' or perhaps, 'If you are interested in jobs in the police, check out this site **www.bluelinejobs.co.uk**'.

Twitter can also be used in a more immediate way at conferences or recruitment events to send out tweets offering to meet recruiters who are looking for candidates.

See the *Guardian's* guide to the top careers people to follow on Twitter. You also get to follow other tweeters and there are many out there offering job-search advice. For instance you can follow @DrJimBright (Jim's tweets) (http:/careers.theguardian.com/careers-blog/careers-advice-top-people-follow-twitter and @DavidAWinter (David's)!

The usual rules apply to Twitter and similar sites like Foursquare, and that is be cautious about requests to meet, verify people's credentials, or go with an experienced friend, and do not switch on the location information option that can reveal to people exactly where you are and where you live. An article by a journalist in *The Guardian* in 2010 demonstrated how easy it was to track down and meet a person, who ironically turned out to be a recruiter, by following the trail of personal and location information she had posted using these sorts of services.

The goal of Twitter is probably summed up best by its CEO, Evan Williams: 'It tells people what they care about as it is happening in the world.'

Networking is giving

A lot of people recoil from the prospect of having to network with others. In the same way they do not like to blow their trumpets about their achievements, they see networking as, in some way, using other people to achieve one's own goals.

We think this is not a good way to think of networking. Instead, we think that good networkers give rather than take. A good networker is someone who listens or reads carefully what other people's needs or interests are. Then they are in a position to be potentially useful to that other person, perhaps by providing them with something that is helpful and relevant to them. For instance, good networkers:

- email relevant news stories
- send copies or details of books of interest
- pass on links to interesting websites
- keep in touch and up to date
- send or relay praise for any achievements or anniversaries
- act like a thoughtful friend.

Consider the list above – all these acts are selfless acts designed to help the other person. None of them is about gaining a personal benefit, let alone a job. Most people would have no difficulty in behaving like that to another, it is simply being friendly and useful. The networking aspect is that in behaving in this manner you are nurturing a reputation as a friendly and useful person. Employment arises when another person has use of your services. Employees who are preferred are those who can be useful to the employer and friendly at the same time.

By seeing networking as an opportunity to make some new friends and to be useful to people, most job hunters become a lot more relaxed about networking, because the chances are they are already doing it without realising it.

The myth of the hidden job market

One final point to make is that going online with your CV and reputation is a form of advertising yourself. Equally, employers have never found it easier or cheaper to advertise jobs. Nearly all jobs are advertised somewhere, contrary to popular belief, and probably the majority are on a website somewhere. The oft-quoted figure of 80 per cent of jobs not being advertised just does not stack up when you consider that, according to

Civil Service statistics in November 2009, there were 5.8 million publicly employed people out of 29 million in the workforce. That is nearly 20 per cent, and just about every one of those jobs is advertised somewhere by regulation. For the 80 per cent figure to be true, it would mean that no other employer advertises, which is total nonsense.

However, the use of advertising will vary from industry to industry. For some sectors, the norm is national advertising. For others they may rely mainly on certain recruitment agencies. In another sector, speculative applications may be the standard way people get jobs. Find out what is appropriate for the sector you want to work in.

In an informal survey of over 5,000 people taking part in the Careers and Employability MOOC run by The Careers Group, University of London, over 40% of people found their most recent job through their personal or professional network.

It is true that many people do not rely solely on job advertisements and use their networks and so, if you have followed all the advice in this book up until the last chapter, we recommend you follow the advice in this chapter too to maximise the chances of your CV landing you that job, so get CASTING!

CHAPTER 19

Internet sites and other resources

The internet is a great tool to search for jobs, post your CV, get some career tips and find out more about the companies you are interested in applying to. We debated about providing Web addresses because of the high turnover of sites, so please accept our apologies in advance if any of the information has changed. When searching for jobs, you can start with a general search term such as 'marketing jobs UK'. However, the more specialised terms you can include in your search, the more likely you are to uncover vacancies related to your experience. So, if you are particularly interested in digital marketing jobs that focus on analysis of metrics, you can use 'digital marketing metrics jobs uk' as your search term. Because similar jobs may have different job titles in different organisations, it may be useful to compile a list of alternative job titles you come across so that you can add them to your search routine. You could also include search terms related to specific skills required in the job as these are less likely to change.

For some resources to help you in your job and advertisement research, check out the following sites.

Trade specific

www.careerstructure.com	Engineering, building trade
www.justengineers.net	Engineering
www.jobsgopublic.com	Public sector
www.gamesindustry.biz	Games industry
www.earthworks-jobs.com	Environmental jobs
www.education-jobs.co.uk	Education

www.tesjobs.co.uk	Teaching and education
www.caterer.com	Catering industry
www.retailchoice.com	Retail
www.jobs.ac.uk	Research, science and academic
www.aquent.co.uk	Digital and marketing communications
www.jobs.nhs.uk	National Health Service
www.computing.co.uk/jobs	IT professional, computing and computer programmer
www.bluelinejobs.co.uk	Police and criminal justice
www.planetrecruit.co.uk	IT, engineering and telecoms

Graduate sites

http://targetjobs.co.uk
www.prospects.ac.uk
www.milkround.com
www.insidecareers.co.uk
www.grb.uk.com
www.gradsintocareers.co.uk
www.graduate-jobs.com
http://graduatetalentpool.direct.gov.uk
www.step.org.uk

Check out your own university careers website for other relevant resources.

General sites

www.jobserve.com
www.jobsite.co.uk
www.stepstone.com
www.monster.co.uk
www.totaljobs.com
www.manpower.com
http://jobs.guardian.co.uk
www.careerjet.co.uk
www.c2careers.com *(offers careers, application and interview coaching)*
www.brightandassociates.com.au *(offers careers direction coaching service via phone and email)*

Jobs overseas

www.jobbankinfo.org
www.mycareer.com.au
www.recruitersonline.com
www.seek.com.au

Government sites

www.governmentjobsdirect.co.uk
www.civilservice.gov.uk/recruitment
www.lgjobs.com

Now it's your turn

Using the examples in Chapter 16 as templates, you are now ready to complete your own CV. Go to it!

Blank templates to photocopy (enlarge to suit)

Template 1: Training template

Secondary/higher education		Dates attended	From	To
Subjects studied	Results	Teams or clubs	Achievements	

Template 2: Jobs template

Employer 1

Employer name and address		Dates attended	From	To
Reason for leaving employer				
Job title	Dates	Key duties	Achievements/promotions	
Training undertaken Title	Instructor/ organisation	Date	Description What I learned	

Employer 2

Employer name and address		Dates attended	From	To
Reason for leaving employer				
Job title	Dates	Key duties	Achievements/promotions	
Training undertaken Title	Instructor/ organisation	Date	Description What I learned	

Template 3: Life template

Activity	Date	Description	Achievements/personal development	Relevance to job applied for
Community				
Work				
Hobbies/interests				
Sports				
Other				

CV howlers!

We asked a bunch of recruitment consultants to give us some examples of really terrible CVs – brilliant disasters in fact. Here is what they said.

brilliant disaster

The ransom note

'One was like a ransom note – letters and words cut out of the newspaper and stuck onto a sheet of paper.'

The self-important scientist going for a non-science job

'A scientist sent in a massive document about two centimetres thick with all their publications in it.'

The runner-up

'One had a load of sports certificates including their school high jump certificate – they hadn't even won. It was for second place!'

Bodily fluids?

'One with dog-eared corners that looked as though the dog had chewed it or the baby had vomited on it.'

'Another with stains – where are the stains from?'

The work of art

'The desktop-published ones for advertising roles. Graphic designers are wonderful – they produce works of art that are like a sample of their work.'

'Personal photos taken in a photo booth. Ghastly.'

The stripper

'One listener phoned into a talkback interview we were giving and told the authors about the man who had his CV hand-delivered by a strippergram.'

Chequepoint Charlie

'A bank manager made his CV out to look like a bank cheque, with the address appearing like the bank's address, and the telephone numbers as the cheque numbers.'

The highrise CV

'An architect produced a 3-D CV that was the perfect model of a house. On lifting the roof, each room contained different information on the candidate.'

One size fits all

'An applicant applied for every general manager's position advertised at the same company, regardless of the functional area, and sent the same poorly typed standard (photocopied) letter of application plus a CV with a "handwritten" reference to the position he was seeking.'

For employers who have trouble reading the fine print

'An applicant sent his entire CV in 16-point font so that it read like a kid's book.'

A little too much information

'This applicant felt the need to share all his secrets, including details of his haemorrhoids.'

Where am I?

'The applicant got the job title wrong (and we mean completely wrong) and then tailored the application to this wrong job.'